WIND-SCULPTED SNOW ALONG WEBB BAY, NORTHERN LABRADOR

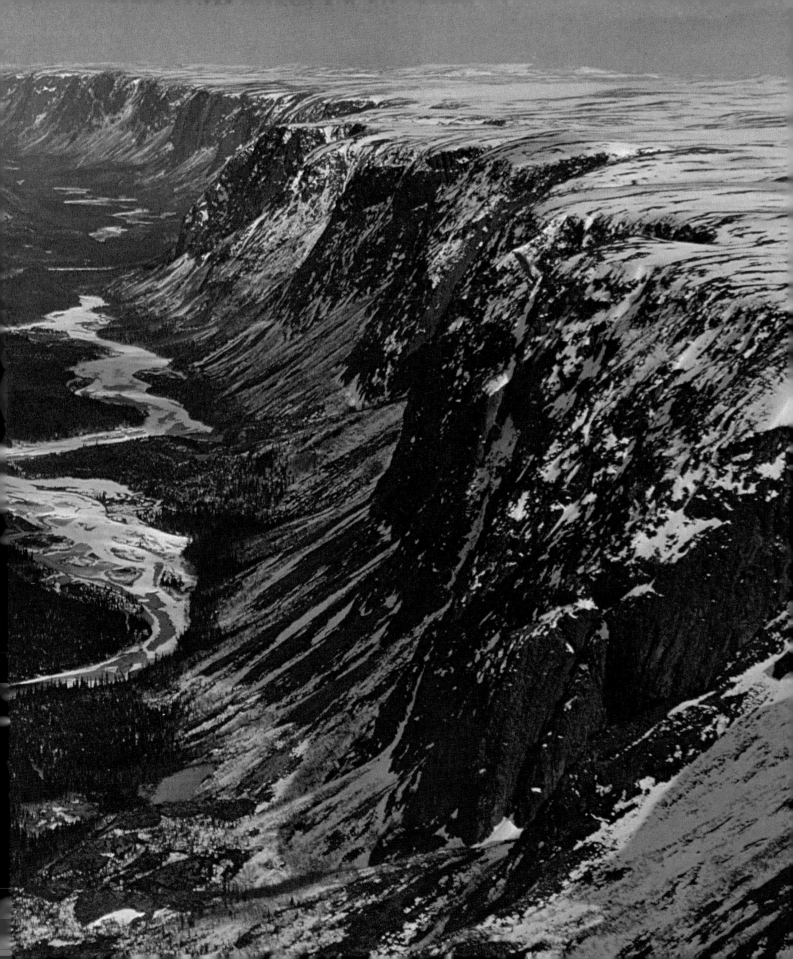

CARIBOU MOSS AND TREES AT THE EDGE OF THE TUNDRA

SUMMER SUNSET ON VOISEY BAY

CARIBOU GATHERING FOR THE OCTOBER BREEDING SEASON

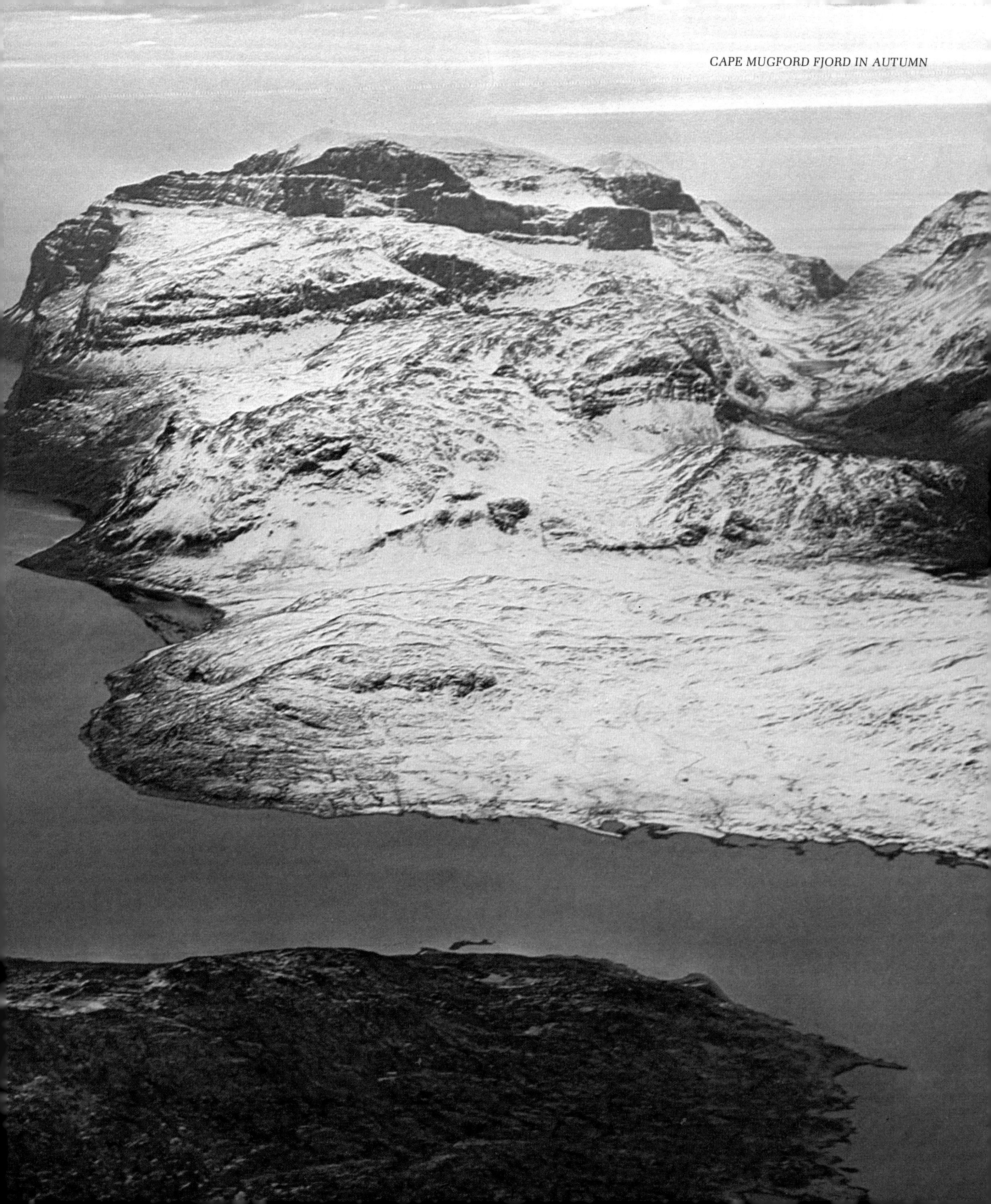

CAPE MUGFORD FJORD IN AUTUMN

TIME
LIFE
BOOKS

LABRADOR

THE WORLD'S WILD PLACES/TIME-LIFE BOOKS/AMSTERDAM

BY ROBERT STEWART

AND THE EDITORS OF TIME-LIFE BOOKS

THE WORLD'S WILD PLACES

EUROPEAN EDITOR: Dale Brown
Deputy Editor: Simon Rigge
Picture Editor: Pamela Marke
Design Consultant: Louis Klein
Staff Writers:
Michael Brown, Norman Kolpas
Art Director: Graham Davis
Designer: Joyce Mason
Picture Researcher: Karin Pearce
Picture Assistant: Thelma Gilbert
Production Staff: Ellen Brush, Molly Sutherland

Editorial Staff For Labrador:
Editor: A. B. C. Whipple
Staff: Neil Kagan, Mary Kay Moran,
Albert Sherman, Elaine Zeitsoff

Published by Time-Life International (Nederland) B.V.
Ottho Heldringstraat 5, Amsterdam 1018.

The Author: The Canadian writer Robert Stewart grew up in an isolated village in the wilderness of north-west Ontario. Now a resident of Montreal, he takes every opportunity to return to his first love, the north woods. He first travelled to Labrador in 1970, and has returned many times since. For this book he spent three months covering thousands of miles of Labrador by aeroplane, coastal vessel, canoe, snowmobile, dogsled and on foot (or snowshoes). His expeditions took him from Cartwright in the south to the Torngat Mountains in the north, and from Makkovik on the coast to Labrador City deep in the interior. A former correspondent and writer for *The Wall Street Journal* and *Time*'s Canadian Edition, he is a frequent contributor to magazines in Canada and the U.S.

The Book Consultant: Sidney Horenstein has been on the staff of the American Museum of Natural History since 1960. He also teaches geology at Hunter College, City University of New York, and is Associate Editor of *Fossils* Magazine. He has served as a consultant on several TIME-LIFE books.

Contents

1/ The Ice-Carved Coast   20

Shapes of a Tortured Land   36

2/ Coping with Labrador's Winter   48

A Flowering Moment of Glory   64

3/An Ill-Fated Expedition   78

A Trek Along the River   98

4/ The Little Creatures   108

5/ An Eloquent Observer   120

Audubon's "Feathered Musicians"   136

6/ Between Forest and Tundra   150

An Armada of Ice   170

Bibliography   180

Acknowledgements and Credits   181

Index   182

A Landscape Sculpted by Glaciers

Located in the north-easternmost corner of North America (light green rectangle on map above), Labrador is politically a section of Newfoundland and geographically part of the Labrador Peninsula, which it shares with the Province of Quebec. Its majestic wilderness encompasses four main vegetation zones. The southernmost area (dark green on map, right) is open mixed forest, which thins out to coniferous forest (light green) in central Labrador and gives way to the area of stunted open woodland (light brown) at the edge of the tundra. Northern Labrador (dark brown) is tundra, where no trees grow.
Among the notable features of the landscape are deep fjords, especially in the area north of Nain. Glaciers have also supplied plunging rivers and large lakes, while in the north rise the mile-high peaks of the Torngat Mountains. The largest man-made mark is the Smallwood Reservoir, a complex of lakes in the western area that supplies power to southern Canada.

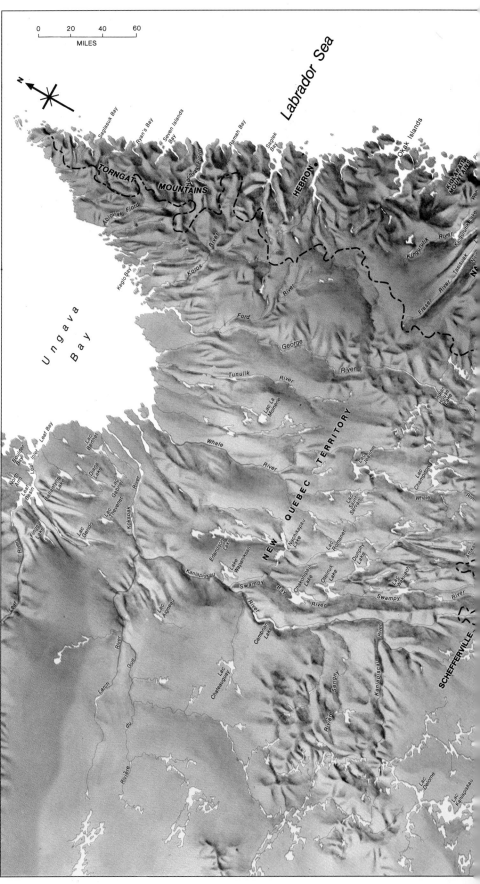

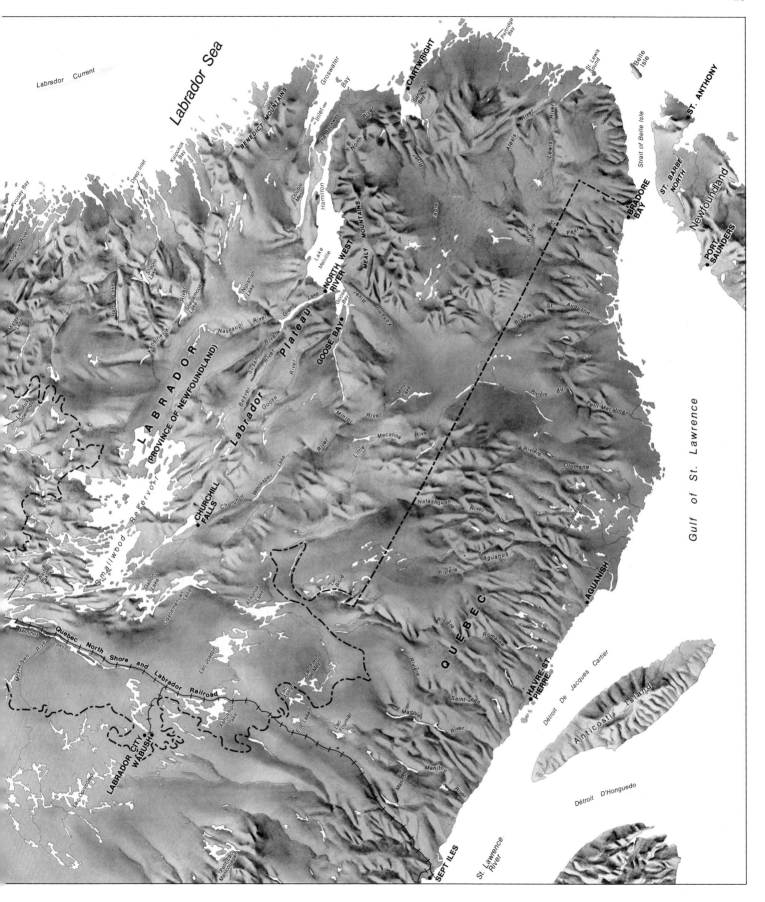

Labrador Sea

Labrador Current

Labrador Current

BENEDICT MOUNTAINS

Voisey Bay

Kogaluk River

Deep Inlet

Kaipokok Bay

Kanairiktok River

Harp Lake

Shapio Lake

Snegamook Lake

Mistastin Lake

Naskaupi River

Grand Lake

Lake Melville

Double Mer

Hamilton

Groswater Bay

Inlet

Traverspine

North River

River

Kenamu River

Goose Bay

Grosswater Bay

Sandwich Bay

CARTWRIGHT

Partridge Bay

River

Alexis

Lewis

St. Lewis Sound

Belle Isle

Strait of Belle Isle

ST. ANTHONY

Newfoundland

ST. BARBE NORTH

PORT SAUNDERS

Eagle

Rivière

St. Paul

BRADORE BAY

St. Augustin

L A B R A D O R

(PROVINCE OF NEWFOUNDLAND)

Labrador Plateau

NORTH WEST RIVER

GOOSE BAY

MEALY MOUNTAINS

Beaver

Susan River

Goose River

Naskaupi River

Kanairiktok River

Smallwood Reservoir

Lac à la Goelette

Ashuanipi Lake

Winokapau Lake

Churchill River

CHURCHILL FALLS

Gabbro Lake

Ossokmanuan Lake

Minipi Lake

Minipi River

Minipi

Little

Mecatina

River

Mecatina River

Natashquan

River

Rivière du

Petit-Mecatina

Rivière

Olomane

Rivière

Aguanus

Rivière

Romaine

AGUANISH

Lac Nipissis

Lac Biolé

Atikonak Lake

Menihek Lakes

McPhadyen River

Quebec

North Shore and Labrador Railroad

Ashuanipi River

Lac Joseph

Eric Lake

Lac Fournier

Lac Josephine

Lac Fleur de May

Q U E B E C

Rivière

Saint-Jean

Magpie River

Rivière

River

HAVRE-ST-PIERRE

Détroit De Jacques Cartier

Anticosti Island

LABRADOR CITY

WABUSH

Lac Opocopa

Lac Ossokmanuan

Rivière

Manitou

Manitou River

Manitou

SEPT ILES

Petit Lac Manicouagan

St. Lawrence River

St. Lawrence River

Gulf of St. Lawrence

Détroit D'Honguedo

1/ The Ice-Carved Coast

God made Labrador in six days. And on the seventh, He threw stones at it. OLD NEWFOUNDLAND SAYING

The islands were in a cluster, at the opposite side of a clear, still bay. They were mostly barren rock, like every other island along this part of the rugged Labrador coast. The only difference was that they appeared to be hanging in the sky, far above the horizon.

Looking at this phenomenon from the deck of the little coastal supply ship *M.V. Nonia*, I thought once again of an observation made to me by an old Labrador hand the first time I came to this beautiful yet forbidding part of the world. "Labrador," he said, "can surprise the hell out of you, you know."

My friend had been referring to Labrador's deceptively "dry cold" weather. "You might not feel too cold," he had warned, "but keep your parka hood tied tight and your mitts on, or you'll wind up with fresh-frozen ears and fingers." In my many visits there since hearing this advice I have realized that this country can surprise the hell out of you in other ways as well—and it was doing so now.

I was looking at a magnificent mirage, as striking as any to be seen in the desert. The islands, although apparently suspended in mid-air, were sharp and clear. The spectacle was caused by differences in the density of the layers of air above the sea, distorting and refracting the light rays so that I was "seeing" an island that was actually below the horizon. Such mirages are common along the Labrador coast, on what local folk call "loomy days", because the images suddenly loom up at them. Sometimes they are upside down. Sometimes the visibility is so good—up to 50 miles—that ships as well as islands can look alarmingly close, although actually they are very long distances away.

Even a map of Labrador is deceptive. The political entity known as Labrador is an annexe of the Canadian province of Newfoundland. But geographically and ecologically the Labrador Peninsula comprises all the coastal area from the entrance to Hudson Bay down to the mouth of the St. Lawrence River (see map pp. 18-19), including a section that is now part of the Province of Quebec. Until the 1920s the entire peninsula was commonly referred to as Labrador.

Still, the area that is now Labrador has enough territory to be a sizeable nation of its own. You could fit the whole of Great Britain into Labrador's 113,000 square miles and have enough room left over for Denmark. Yet you could take Labrador's entire population of about 30,000 to the tennis championships at Wimbledon and still have a few seats left over.

The country has only about 40 year-round villages, approximately as many as there are on a single 15-mile stretch of the south coast of England. On Labrador's far northern coast there are a number of ghost colonies; once Eskimo settlements, they were founded by Moravian missionaries, and so the sites bear such biblical names as Ramah, Zoar and Hebron. In most cases little more than the names remain; the outposts have been abandoned over the years as the missionaries' influence waned and the government relocated the Eskimos. Now the only inhabited settlement in far northern Labrador is Nain: total population fewer than 850. All traces of Ramah and Zoar have long since vanished; Hebron remains a forlorn clutch of deteriorating shacks visited only by an occasional Eskimo family on a hunting or fishing expedition. These empty little places, in a land of dazzling Northern Lights and nocturnal wolf calls, silently testify to Labrador's awful isolation; and to its haunting loneliness. "Lots of ghosts in Hebron," a little black-eyed Eskimo girl once told me; her father did not disagree.

It was in Nain that I had embarked on my voyage aboard the *Nonia*. I had come in by air, on the eight-passenger Otter seaplane that flies up to Nain from Goose Bay twice a week, weather permitting. It was mid-September and Nain had been enjoying Indian summer at its balmiest—the finest weather Canada has to offer anywhere at any time of year.

I took advantage of the mild temperature and the sharp visibility to explore the countryside. At night I rolled up in my sleeping bag in a deserted mission school dormitory. But when I awoke in the morning, I swung my feet down on the wooden floor and felt the sting of cold through my heavy woollen socks. What I had taken for dust on the floor was actually granular snow that had sifted through the broken window panes while I was sleeping. I glanced out at a pewter-grey sky that sent a fresh chill through my body just looking at it. The wind was whipping the snow off the bare black rock and chasing it restlessly about.

When I wrapped myself up and stepped outside, the wind blew my breath behind me in a plume of visible vapour. I had planned to fly back south that morning. So I hurried down the rocky path to the government store-cum-trading post to find out if the change in the weather had delayed the seaplane from Goose Bay. The people in the store told me that it didn't look as if it would be flying today. The storm might blow over here, but a blizzard was raging to the south of us, according to the weather report on the radio. It turned out, however, that I was not stranded. Luckily, *Nonia* was at the dock, unloading winter supplies. I managed to get aboard for the return voyage south to Goose Bay.

Nonia would make the run, if that is the correct word, along the coast to Goose Bay and comparative civilization in four days, stopping at five settlements along this 300-mile stretch of Labrador's coast. I was not unhappy with the change in my plans—provided, of course, that a storm at sea didn't pin us down in some barren harbour of refuge for a week or so. The voyage would offer me an excellent opportunity to study Labrador's craggy coastline and to ride the stormy North Atlantic waters that help make Labrador what it is—one of the world's wildest places, and one of its most imposing and ancient landscapes.

Labrador is at the eastern edge of the geological nucleus of North America—an enormous saucer-shaped mass known as the Canadian Shield, with the depression of Hudson Bay at its centre. The Labrador rim of the gigantic saucer consists of an uneven plateau with peaks rising to more than 5,000 feet. The Canadian Shield is a remarkable geological phenomenon. This mass of granitic rock, some of it dating back nearly four billion years, is one of the oldest areas of exposed rock in the world. Uplifted 800 million years ago by relentless forces deep within the earth, Labrador's landscape has through millions of years been eroded by wind, rain and ice, submerged under the sea and wrenched by continental drift.

A major force that contributed to its character was ice; the remorseless glaciation that moved across Labrador—and as far south as what is now New York City—which scoured and pitted, abraded and tor-

Indicative of Labrador's undeveloped state is the coastal village of Nain, its main street still a rutted road and its cabins huddled against the mountainside. With a population of somewhat fewer than 850, Nain is Labrador's northern metropolis.

tured its surface into the majestic wilderness that still remains today.

The ice made it into a land of tremendous variety. The glaciers rounded and smoothed the rock across wide expanses of plateau. The moving ice also gouged out innumerable shallow depressions that filled with water to form lakes, and cut chasms out of river valleys; the Churchill River drops more than 1,000 feet over a single 16-mile stretch. The glaciers dug deep cirques: circular valleys that end in sheer cliffs dropping sharply into U-shaped valleys. And along the coast the grinding mass of ice carved still larger valleys that, when it at last melted and raised the sea level, became steep fjords indenting the Labrador coastline.

The crushing weight of a glacial ice sheet, more than a mile high in some areas, also forced much of Labrador's surface down into the earth's mantle. And when the ice finally retreated, the land lifted again, as much as 600 feet in parts of its interior. Many miles inland there still are fossilized shells and other evidence that this high plateau country once was sea bottom, before the land rose above the spreading seas.

The extreme topography is in the north: there the Torngat Mountains rise more than 5,000 feet—so high that their peaks poked above the last ice sheet 18,000 years ago. The mountainous terrain of the north turns into hilly country as you move south; the landscape there is much less forbidding. Where all is rock and treeless tundra in the north, the boreal forest clothes the land from Labrador's midsection south to the Gulf of St. Lawrence.

This formidable country is virtually impenetrable by normal means. In all of Labrador there are only two highways, and the great bulk of the area has no roads at all. The only way to see most of it is from the air. Droning over this seemingly limitless expanse of wilderness, you can watch the different ecosystems merge into one another: from the open mixed forests growing in the southern third of Labrador to the coniferous forest in the colder midsection; thence to the no-man's land between forest and subarctic tundra, with its mixture of stunted trees and swampy alpine meadow; and finally to the Arctic tundra itself covered for most of the year by snow and supporting little more than willow bushes, low sedges and that hardy lichen called caribou moss.

Even from a plane you can see the spectacular effects of glaciation and weathering: the rocky debris left by the gouging ice, with house-sized boulders perched on top of hills where they were deposited by the glaciers; the giant fissures and fractures that have been widened by the interminable wear of water and ice; the tortured upthrusts of rock that has been twisted and folded upon itself; and the steep-walled fjords chiselled deep into the coastline.

Another clear impression of Labrador from the air is that it remains virtually unchanged by man. In spite of the technology that has made possible tunnels through the Alps and super highways across deserts, it still is extremely difficult to run a reliable transportation system in Labrador, if only because of its frigid and blustery climate through most of the year. As long as goods and people cannot be moved from place to place with regularity, this wilderness will remain out of bounds to all but the hardiest human beings.

A person must be tough psychologically as well as physically to live here. The very few companies with operations in Labrador—mostly mining and logging—have a chronic problem with employees who gradually develop isolation neurosis; in the Labrador vernacular, they get "bushed". The bleakness of their lives and the constant assaults of nature are disorientating. Labrador is buffeted by cold air masses charging in from the Labrador Sea on the east and from Hudson Bay on the west. In the interior the average temperature in February is 10°F below zero. But that's not all. The winds howling in from Hudson Bay can combine with subarctic temperatures to drive the wind-chill factor to the equivalent of more than 100°F below zero. In such conditions even the most experienced trappers regularly suffer frostbite.

Adding to winter's hazards is the phenomenon called a "white-out", in which a combination of wind-blown snow and light refracting from it reduces visibility to nil. During a white-out, a man can walk smack into a tree or lose his way and travel in circles without knowing it. Even moving a relatively short distance—from one building to another—a man can so lose his way that he succumbs to the bitter cold and freezes to death. Sustained exposure to a white-out can also damage the eyes. Animals deal wisely with the problem: if they can find the slightest shelter, they lie down, close their eyes and do not move.

Nonetheless, there are plenty of clear, bright days of "dry cold"; they can be quite agreeable if you are properly dressed for sub-zero weather. And bad weather can dramatically change to good; for instance, within a few hours of waking up shivering in Nain that day, I was sunning myself in shirtsleeves on *Nonia's* deck.

The air had a crystalline brilliance and its purity seemed to make breathing a treat. We were in sheltered waters, moving among a maze of rock islands that had been eroded by glaciers into gently reclining shapes. This "drowned shore" is so called because the islands are the tops of hills that once were entirely above water and now are partly submerged after the melting of glacial ice. From the air the view looks like a jigsaw puzzle strewn along a carpet. At twilight on this fine day the islands turned a gorgeous pale pink. But I realized that I should savour the scene while I could, for soon enough we would be out in the wild Labrador Sea.

By the next afternoon we were in open water and the surging waves began to buffet the ship. I could not help thinking about the Norsemen who had first come here. By modern standards *Nonia* is a small vessel— about 1,200 tons. When you are rocking in the ferocious waters off Cape Harrison, that does not seem nearly big enough. But at least *Nonia* had engines to drive her along and her stout iron plates provided warm shelter below decks. The Norsemen, by contrast, sailed these waters in ships about half *Nonia*'s size. The Norse vessel, about 60 feet long and only partly decked, fore and aft, was called a *knarr*. The decks protected the cargo and cattle; the crew spent most of the time in the open, exposed to the storms of the Labrador Current. Whenever the winds moderated, the *knarr*'s coarse woollen sail, or *wadmal*, could be raised. The vessel's only other means of propulsion was the crew itself; the oarsmen pulled on long sweeps extending through holes cut in the uppermost planks of the *knarr*. It is difficult to imagine such a craft surviving in winds reaching 50 to 60 knots, as they often do on the Labrador Sea. It is not so difficult to imagine the crew's discomfort; but it helps to spend a quarter of an hour out on the deck of any ship in the Labrador Sea during such a blow. For a Norseman skimpily clad in a spume-soaked woollen gown, straining on an oar, it must have been a truly terrible experience.

The Norsemen came to Labrador, but they didn't stay. The first to arrive was Biarni Heriulfson. Heriulfson thought nothing of crossing the Atlantic in his open boat every autumn to trade with the settlers in Iceland, including his father, Heriulf. In the year 986 Heriulfson found that his father had joined a group, led by Eric the Red, who had gone to explore and settle Greenland. Heading for Greenland, Heriulfson found himself off the Labrador coast. "It appears to me that this is worthless country," Labrador's discoverer is quoted in the Icelandic Sagas; and he set out to find his father in Greenland.

Along the coast Labrador looks no more inviting today than it did 10 centuries ago. There are no modern amenities; nor are there any monuments, souvenir stands or tourist buses.

Already speckled with snow in autumn, a stretch of "drowned shore", mountains once exposed but now partly covered by water from melted glaciation, projects from the southern coast of the Labrador Peninsula near the Strait of Belle Isle.

A major guardian of this wilderness is the Labrador Current. Composed of frigid waters from the Arctic Ocean, it pours down from the top of the world, chilling all the air above it. It flows ceaselessly at about half a mile an hour, 1,300 feet deep and 10 to 20 miles across, and powerfully influences all forms of life on the north-east edge of the Atlantic Ocean. The Labrador Current gives the coast its basic ecological character: an environment of plant, animal and marine life that has adapted to the cold. Yet in spite of its frigid effect on the climate, its overall influence is a positive one. It brings a great bounty to the coast; and although its storms are feared by seamen, on balance it is a giver, more than a taker, of life.

The Current is rich in mineral salts that are swept up from the floor of the Arctic Ocean. On its way south the Current collects more nutrients—other minerals, plankton, krill—in the Davis Strait and along the coast of West Greenland. They nourish masses of microscopic planktonic plants, which in turn feed countless zooplankton. Throughout its length, then, the Current feeds the fishes of the Labrador Coast.

It sends a stream eastwards to meet the warm, northbound Gulf Stream, whereupon the waters explode with fresh life as the plankton thrives and multiplies. Small fish such as capelin, herring, young cod and haddock feast off this effusion. They in turn are feasted upon by adult cod, pollack, haddock, mackerel, halibut and other species. These fish are eaten by sharks and swordfish, whales and seals, and all kinds of sea birds. And all, of course, are eaten by man. The Grand Banks of Newfoundland, where the Labrador Current and the Gulf Stream meet, provide one of the great commercial fishing areas of the world.

The clash of temperatures, as the cold and warm currents converge, also makes this one of the world's foggiest places. The air above the Labrador Current is so cold that the warmer air coming north over the Gulf Stream condenses just as steam from a bathtub does when it hits a cold piece of glass. The brunt of the Current is aptly called "the cold wall". It is a thin wall, as was demonstrated by a measurement once taken by the U.S. Coast Guard frigate *Tampa*. The crew took the water temperature at the bow and at the stern simultaneously as the small vessel straddled the line where the Current and the Gulf Stream make head-on contact. At the bow the water temperature was 33°F; at the stern, 56°F. The air temperature contrast has also been measured, and differences of as much as 50°F have been recorded at points only five miles apart. In summer, the clash of temperatures causes dense fog to reign in the area of the cold wall about 40 per cent of the time.

The persistent fog is navigational menace enough; but the Labrador Current is also what sailors call "Iceberg Alley". Each year the Current carries thousands of bergs down from the High North. It was a Labrador Current iceberg that sank the *Titanic* in 1912. Scores of smaller ships have also been sunk, on the Grand Banks fishing grounds and on the heavily-trafficked sea lanes south of Newfoundland, by icebergs brought south by the Labrador Current.

An iceberg is a thing of menace but also of breathtaking beauty. I gasped at my first sight of one close up. I had just come on to the deck of *Nonia* and found myself looking at an iceberg just a few hundred feet away. It was as if some omnipotent benefactor had delivered the Taj Mahal to me as a surprise gift.

We had come out of the open ocean into calmer water. The iceberg swayed gracefully from side to side. The bright morning sun glinted on its turquoise-white twin domes. A pale blue halo seemed to limn its contours against the deeper blue of the sky. I could see how the icy beauty of diamonds presents such a mesmerizing attraction. The top of this berg was like a floating cache of jewels. There were also rough ridges of ice ringing the glittering mass, in spirals rising up from its base, and they stood out like shimmering strings of pearls. It was not, I was later informed, a very big iceberg. But it was the first I had ever seen; it was plenty big enough, and it was mine.

I was fascinated to discover, from veteran iceberg watchers, that these massive jewels strung along Labrador's coast are as deceptive in their way as Labrador itself. An iceberg is not the still and silent dead-weight one would expect; far from it. Schools of fish swim under and around each floating mass of ice, feeding on the plankton attached to its base and submerged sides. Whales are sometimes seen holding station with an iceberg, attracted by the fish. Birds perch on the translucent blue crags, rising to wheel and dive for the fish near the surface. The iceberg itself seems alive—turning with the current, rolling with its changing weight and dislodging huge chunks of ice that thunder into the water. As an iceberg disintegrates, it produces a noise like hailstones beating on a roof. Often a melting iceberg miles away can be heard before it can be seen, even on relatively fog-free days.

Mariners give icebergs a wide berth. Skippers who know the waters off Labrador also know that you can never judge the course of a berg by the direction of the wind. Only about one-tenth of the icy mass rides above the surface of the water. The cumbrous underbelly is steered by

Like a floating snowman, an iceberg moves down Labrador's northern coast. The dots on its surface are kittiwakes (opposite page).

deep ocean currents that can be 180 degrees different from the surface current. Since an iceberg is generally shaped like an inverted mushroom, with the tip of its stem poking above the water, a ship can collide with the underwater part while still well removed from the visible portion. Moreover, a berg can turn turtle with a thunderous splash that sends enormous waves outwards for miles.

When I disembarked from *Nonia* and returned home, I did some reading about the origins of icebergs. I found that my iceberg probably came from the west coast of Greenland, where some 7,000 of them drop into the Labrador Current each year. This accounts for about 70 per cent of all the icebergs in the Labrador Sea; the rest come from Ellesmere, Baffin and the other Canadian Arctic islands. Icebergs from the opposite coast of Greenland are usually melted by the warm Irminger Current as they round the tip of Greenland, although some of the larger ones may survive to move down the Labrador coast.

Gazing enthralled at that swaying, sighing jewel of the sea, I was aware that I was looking at a remnant of one of the great events in the earth's history. Until it splashed into the water a thousand miles north of us, this iceberg was a tangible part of the latest (but not necessarily the last) Ice Age. It was once an infinitesimal bit of the massive ice sheet that to this day covers the entire interior of Greenland—more than a million square miles of it, up to 11,000 feet thick and weighing several thousand million tons per square mile.

It was this fantastic weight that had set my iceberg in motion. Great glaciers formed and started moving through the coastal mountains. The Humboldt Glacier on Smith Isthmus, for example, has a front of 68 miles. It meets the water of Davis Strait as a solid wall of ice 292 feet high. But the front wall of a glacier is not really solid. Although the foot of it does not seem to move, it is in constant motion internally. Glacial ice has been compacted from the snowfalls of many years and consists of layers of fairly large and regular crystals that flatten out and slip against one another like cards in a loose deck. The glacier also tends to melt a bit as the result of warmth generated by the downward pressure of the ice pack. So, near its base, a glacier is capable of sliding.

As the weight of the ice pack pushes the front wall down and outwards, the glacier moves—without appearing to move at all. It moves irregularly, usually a few miles a month but sometimes in a surge of 20 miles a day, as it travels down a valley towards one of the fjords of Western Greenland. And as it travels, it tears chunks out of the rock beneath it. The unevenness of the rock base in turn causes the ice to

Skirting the edges of the iceberg (opposite), a kittiwake hovers while looking for food. These gulls are resting on the berg during their migration to northern Labrador and Greenland for the summer breeding season.

crack; in addition the glacier is fractured by the shape of the terrain, and the central part of the glacier usually moves faster than the ice flowing down the sides of the valley. Thus a glacier reaches the sea with yawning vertical fissures, spaced at intervals. It rides down the slope to the sea, pushed from behind by the immense weight of ice. In the water the currents rasp at its bottom. Tides jostle it up and down. All these forces cause huge chunks of ice to snap off and tumble into the water. In this way an iceberg is "calved".

Hardly calf-sized, some icebergs are as tall as 10-storey buildings, and that is only the one-tenth that is visible. Although there have been reports of mile-long icebergs, most are about a third of a mile. An iceberg can weigh several million tons, and it rides along in the Labrador Current at about 20 nautical miles a day.

My own iceberg was probably a two-year-old, calved in summer. It would have moved out to the northern part of Baffin Bay by autumn. There the freeze-up would have trapped it until the following spring. By spring it probably drifted southwards throughout the summer, to reach Cape Dyer or the Hudson Strait, where it again was locked in for the winter. In the succeeding spring it resumed its southward journey.

Meanwhile it had melted steadily. A berg that weighs one and a half million tons in Baffin Bay will be reduced to 150,000 tons—still a formidable weight—by the time it passes south of Newfoundland. Gradually it shrinks in size, rolling and splashing as its balance shifts. Some icebergs produce progeny as they themselves are calved, splitting apart as if cleaved by a giant axe. Only a fraction of the total number of icebergs calved in Greenland and the Arctic islands ever clear the bottom of Newfoundland to imperil transatlantic shipping. Many of them melt away in the bays of Labrador and Newfoundland. Others die in the warm waters of the Gulf Stream. As they melt, the rock and earth that they picked up as glaciers sink to the sea bottom. The Grand Banks, a huge Atlantic Ocean shoal of the North American continent, is veneered with deposits from melted icebergs.

Icebergs are visible reminders of an Ice Age that ended in Labrador only 7,000 years ago—a mere tick of the clock in the measurement of geological time. An ice age seems like something slightly this side of science fiction: it takes an effort of imagination to picture New York City and London smothered under a mile-high sheet of ice. But in Labrador, only 900 miles from New York, an ice age does not seem at all remote; there, mementoes of the most recent Ice Age are visible all around

In a feeding flurry, kittiwakes plunge after fish

and plankton under an iceberg (page 30). Unlike other gulls, kittiwakes not only dive for their food but can also swim under water.

Along the Canairitock River, the slower-moving water inside each turn has piled up alluvial debris along the bank.

you. Flying up the coast, you can look down on a capsized iceberg floating belly-up with a few big rocks embedded in its base. Just such rock in just such ice carved the face of Labrador. Sail down one of Labrador's steep-cliffed fjords and you are following a trench bulldozed out of the rock by an Ice Age glacier. Look at the rock islands that abound along the coast and you are viewing the hilltops of land once depressed by the weight of glaciation and then submerged as the melting ice poured thousands of millions of gallons of icy water into the sea. Walk along a trail in the interior forest and look up at a near-by hill; there, sitting incongruously on top of it, is an enormous round boulder. It is what geologists term an "erratic"—a rock that shouldn't be where it is, but was dumped there by a melting glacier.

When you are snowshoeing along a Labrador trail in midwinter, with the sub-zero wind lashing your face, it is difficult to believe that this was once a warm place all year round. But more than 100,000 years ago, scientists say, there was rich, thick soil here; wild horses grazed on its grasses; peccaries, the forerunners of domestic pigs, rooted among the trees. In this beneficent era, called the Sangamonian Interglacial Stage, the climate of Labrador was like that of southern Germany today.

But climatic changes gradually brought an end to the Sangamonian interval. In the tens of thousands of years that have followed, Labrador has been overwhelmed by ice again and again. The combined effect—particularly the scouring and gouging of the moving ice masses—completed the job that erosion had started on the face of Labrador millions of years earlier. Besides forming the rivers and lakes, the valleys and fjords, it exposed the ancient rock. The Canadian Shield is Precambrian, which means that it is more than 600 million years old. It is by far the largest exposed area of Precambrian rock in the world. Some of it dates back 2,900 million years. In comparison, the Himalayas are a mere 70 million years old. For me this provides a small sense of personal satisfaction. I enjoy thinking that, while others have climbed higher peaks in Europe or Asia, in Labrador I have climbed a hill that is 1,500 million years old.

Shapes of a Tortured Land

Few areas of the earth reflect their tortured evolution so dramatically as does Labrador. The landscape, as raw today as in its prehistoric infancy, manifests the convulsive development that began nearly four thousand million years ago.

After the molten globe began to cool, a crust formed over the seething mantle. Irresistible forces within the hot depths—known as convection currents—pushed up mountains on the earth's surface. In the area that is now Labrador, erosion began to wear away these mountains. Meanwhile, more movements within the earth caused the eroding land to sink.

The sea washed in over these depressed areas; various types of sediment drifted down to the sea floor; the lower layers were compressed into rock. And more stirrings in the earth's mantle exerted such pressure and heat on these sedimentary rocks that the ones near the bottom were changed into more durable metamorphic rock.

Again came massive internal convulsions; again mountains rose and the sea retreated, and erosion exposed the sedimentary and metamorphic rocks. In fact, this sequence occurred four times in a span of 3,500 million years. During the fourth sequence, however, the convection currents unaccountably did not further compress the sedimentary rock, but merely raised it again above sea level. And this time erosion wore away the sedimentary rock, exposing the harder, underlying metamorphic rock of the three previous upheavals. Since that time erosion has exceeded uplift in the Labrador area; thus parts of its terrain still look much as they did 3,500 million years ago.

They look similar, that is, in texture but not in shape—because of two more assaults on the landscape in the north-east region of the continent. About 200 million years ago the convection currents pushed a gigantic area 5,000 feet into the air, and then pulled it apart. The sea filled the gap, forming two land masses. One is Labrador, the other Greenland. Even today the seaside cliffs facing each other could almost fit together like pieces of a jigsaw.

The most recent assault, 17,000 years ago, was glaciation, which carved and etched all of Labrador's landscape (*pages 40-47*). The result of all these forces—immersion, upheaval, glaciation and other erosion—is a starkly beautiful landscape.

Along Labrador's coast, erosion continues its work. Rocks crumbled into detritus at the base will eventually cover this mountain.

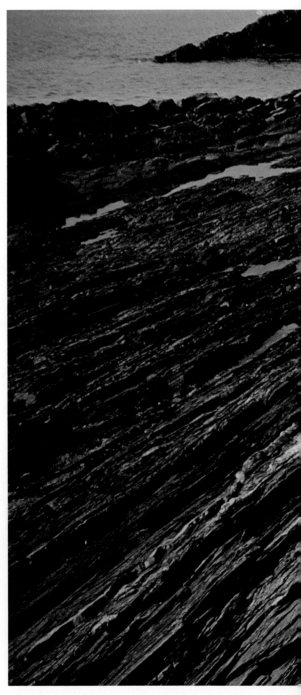

Originally layers of sand at the bottom
of the sea, the metamorphic rock above
preserves even the ripples of the former
surface. Erosion has worn away the
less durable sedimentary rock that
formed above it and what remains is
a rugged shelf lying along the shore.

Millions of years of erosion and the
more recent battering of the sea have
exposed the original patterns of this
metamorphic rock (right) on Labrador's
north-east coast. With the weaker rock
layers etched away, the stronger
rock stands out in relief.

A Topography Smoothed by Ice

Massive glaciers moved over the surface of Labrador during four ice ages in a period of a million years. A glacier is at once a giant bulldozer, a file and a sled. The glaciers smoothed the peaks and flanks of Labrador's mountains, and carried the detritus hundreds of miles away, to dump it when the ice finally melted. Labrador's valleys were broadened and deepened; high-hanging ravines were carved out of cliffsides; deep fjords were formed. Thus the present rolling topography of Labrador, shown here and on the following pages, was created.

Since the glaciers' retreat, erosion has continued, abetted along the coastline by other forces of nature. The battering of the sea and inundations of tides have carved the rock, in some areas grinding it to sand, which in turn has drifted out and raised the sea floor.

Today the glaciers have retreated to the Arctic. But still the forces of erosion continue; and like a living thing, Labrador's landscape continues to change—almost imperceptibly, but nevertheless relentlessly.

Rounded by glacial action 17,000 years ago, these rock cliffs along Labrador's northern coast have been carved by ice and the sea. The black streaks once were molten liquid, which invaded the fissures of the rock before it was pushed up from within the crust of the earth more than a thousand million years ago.

Set in a glacier-carved valley beneath
glacier-rounded cliffs, a hollowed-out
cirque marks the area where a later
glacier formed and moved into the sea
(foreground). The gridwork on the
cliffside (right) was made more recently
when water froze inside the rock
fractures and enlarged them. Now the
fractures are filled with snow.

The birth of a fjord can be reconstructed from the view above, looking down a valley that was carved by a glacier. When the ice melted, the sea level rose and water flooded in and submerged the lower end of the ravine.

A hanging valley (left) was created when a glacier deepened its depression above the waterfall, but was forced up and over a resistant ledge. Then, like the waterfall, it moved down to dig another deep valley beneath the first.

Bringing to life visions of the last Ice Ages, fog sweeps through the Torngat Mountains in northern Labrador at about the height of

the last glaciers 17,000 years ago. It was in this area that the land mass of Greenland finally split away from the North American continent.

2/ Coping with Labrador's Winter

On and on they came. Nothing could stop them or make them swerve. The first ones saw us from the water standing up behind our fire. But they came straight on, all the animals racing up the bank to make room for the next lot. They scattered slightly on either side to give us room, and for what seemed an eternity we were surrounded by a sea of caribou.

CAPT. THIERRY MALLET/ *THE BEAVER*

One tends to forget during the long monotone of the winters in Labrador that one of the country's impressive attractions is its variety of climate. The vivid contrasts of the four seasons are the spice of Labrador life—at least, so say those few who live there. The temperature range through the Labrador year goes from minus 60°F to plus 90°F. It's like living at the North Pole and on the Equator all in the same year.

The transitional seasons are a special delight. Spring in Labrador is a brief touch of tenderness after seven months of bitter winter broken only by one or two fleeting thaws. The spring break-up is like a great jail break, heralding a release from days of immobilizing blizzards and too little sunlight, from food shortages, isolation and enforced confinement, and from the heaviness and awkwardness of winter clothing. Spring really *springs* in Labrador.

The ice on the lakes and rivers snaps and shatters, sending torrents of water, brown with sediment, to flood large areas of forest. Trout dart back and forth, rejuvenated by the changing season and a fresh ingestion of oxygen after their sluggish winter under the ice. The ice barrier that has clogged the fjords and closed off the harbours now crumples. Ice pans and icebergs sail south along the coast on the Labrador Current, carrying seals and an occasional polar bear. Inland, among the damp mosses of the forest floor, buds spring up magically. Hungry mother bears go marauding with their cubs, born in their lairs in

January and now at the toddling stage. Hatches of insects attract the birds migrating back north to serenade their forest world.

If spring in Labrador is a spectacular time of change, autumn is even more so. It too is brief, lasting only a month or two; and like spring, it is a release—this time from the sweat of summer and from the constant plague of flies and mosquitoes that are killed by the first frost. In the more southerly areas autumn offers splashes of muted colour. The leaves of the birches and poplars glow like burnished gold, interspersed with the pink of the willows, the purple of the fireweed, the velvety crimson of Labrador Tea, the dark green of the black spruces, and the mustard yellow of the tamaracks. The sunlight softens yet remains warm, bringing long, slow sunsets of mauve and smoky blue.

Autumn in Labrador offers a special ripeness. I was surprised the first time I saw people in Labrador picking blueberries in mid-September; in central Canada the summer heat had long since killed most of the fruit. But Labrador's summer temperatures, while sometimes extremely high, do not remain so for long, and many of the berries ripen late, achieving their full succulence only after a summer of soaking up the gentle sunshine. I picked some myself; they were smaller and paler than the ones I am used to, but full of flavour. The low-lying red partridge berries and the raspberries were equally delicious and they flourished in incredible numbers.

But there is also a special significance to autumn in Labrador: it is the time when its creatures prepare for the long siege of a winter harsher than in most areas of the world. Some simply escape it by migrating south. Others hide from it by sleeping for long periods. Nearly all Labrador's fauna begin in autumn to equip themselves for the cold weather ahead. There is a sense of urgency in their activity; they seem to know instinctively that from the month of September onwards, the Labrador winter can strike at any time.

Throughout the length of the food chain there is a mass stocking-up. Physiological changes begin to take place. Fur and feathers grow heavier and thicker. The ptarmigans exchange their superb summer camouflage of mottled brown for a superb winter camouflage of stark white. The varying, or snowshoe, hare and the weasel similarly begin to change colour. In the weasel each dark hair is replaced by a white one, and there is a midway point when the weasel's coat is an odd salt-and-pepper mixture. Snowshoe hares grow a white coat on top of their soft reddish-grey underfur. The reasons for the changing colours differ as much as the methods. For the hare it provides protection not only from the cold but also from predators. For the predatory weasel the white hair helps it to become an even more efficient hunter in winter—of snowshoe hares, among other prey.

One day late in September I set out to observe the preparations for winter in a Labrador forest. A couple of miles back in the bush from North West River, I found a comfortable hollow under a big, straight birch tree and there sat still for several hours. As I watched, the forest came alive around me. Two spruce grouse startled me with the sudden whirr of their wings as they took off from cover near my tree. A raven cruised across the sky—a shiny black monster big enough to amaze anyone accustomed to the size of ordinary crows. Labrador ravens are scavengers with a fantastic sense of smell, appearing out of nowhere for their share of meat when the wolves kill a caribou. Watching this spooky creature wheeling above me, I reflected that it was no wonder Edgar Allan Poe chose the raven as a symbol of the unknown.

As I sat there, I noticed plenty of activity among the smaller birds, which were pecking seeds out of the caribou moss, the grey, spongy lichen carpeting the forest floor. My chief four-footed companions were squirrels. As dusk began to fall, a couple of flying squirrels began doing their aerial act in the treetops. Actually they should be called "gliding squirrels"; they stretch out the membrane of skin between their front and back legs to keep them aloft like kites. But while they don't really fly, they don't simply spread themselves out and jump, either. Watching closely, I could see them using their tails deliberately to steer and trim themselves. They can turn and twist almost at right angles in mid-flight, to avoid small twigs and branches in their way and to alight on a chosen branch. These squirrels were covering distances of perhaps 50 to 60 feet at a glide. The flying squirrel's lightness contributes to its gliding performance: it rarely weighs more than 3 to 5 ounces. But the squirrel's small size is a hazard, too. Natural enemies such as owls, ravens, hawks, martens and weasels kill off a large proportion of flying squirrels before they are five years old.

That day red squirrels, the flying variety's cousins, were dashing back and forth from the trees to the ground foraging for food. I was interested to observe that they had a fondness for the big orange mushrooms that thrive in the caribou moss. Red squirrels lead even more perilous lives than their flying kin: they have to contend with predators both on the ground and in the trees. Foxes, lynxes and minks go after them, as do flesh-eating hawks and owls and tree-climbing mammals

The ptarmigan of Labrador offers dramatic evidence of climatic adaptation, changing from rich brown to snow-white plumage between summer and winter. Both colours serve as excellent protective camouflage: the mottled brown (lower pictures) blends with the summer foliage; in autumn the bird moults, revealing an undercoat of white (top picture) that blends with winter snow. In spring the ptarmigan grows a new layer of brown feathers.

MALE PTARMIGAN: WINTER PLUMAGE

MALE PTARMIGAN: MOULTING IN AUTUMN

FEMALE PTARMIGAN: SUMMER PLUMAGE

such as martens. Red squirrels can swim, but then they can be swallowed by pike or big trout. These squirrels even pose a danger to one another. They guard their food caches fiercely, and fight to the death against other poaching squirrels. If you see one red squirrel chasing another in the woods, chances are that they are not playing. The one in front has probably been stealing the other's food, and is desperately trying to escape its murderous wrath.

The busy squirrel is too preoccupied during its autumn foraging to be concerned by the presence of man. It not only stores food in its nest, but it also devours a huge amount to build up fat as a defence against the cold. The red squirrel does not hibernate, in the technical sense of the term. Instead it confines itself in its lair for spells of a week or more when the weather is extremely cold.

Its larger relative, the woodchuck, on the other hand, does hibernate. To prepare for its long sleep, the woodchuck eats an amazing amount, up to 17 times its weight, during a few weeks in autumn. Its hibernation is a kind of coma, in which its body temperature is near freezing point and its heartbeat almost stops. The woodchuck loses up to half its weight during this sleep.

I made a small contribution to the winter sustenance of the red squirrel by throwing scraps of my sandwiches on to the ground around my tree. As the blue evening drew darker and the first owl began to hoot, I walked slowly out of the woods.

Squirrels, hares and weasels are among the smaller fauna that stay in Labrador all the year round and adapt in their own way to winter. Among the bigger animals that stay put are the black bear and the moose. In autumn Labrador's bears feed on berries, nuts and seeds and just about anything else they can procure, including the hard-earned food caches of the squirrels—and the squirrels themselves if the bear can move fast enough to catch them. The bears also dig mice out of their nests, raid birds' nests for eggs and baby birds, and gorge themselves on the ants that inhabit the rotten wood of dead trees. They are not averse to carrion, and will feast off any carcass left by a fox or other predator. When the time comes for their winter slumber, the bears are positively rolling in fat.

But, contrary to legend, they do not really hibernate; their body temperature and breathing remain constant. They do, however, sleep soundly for lengthy periods. It is difficult to wake a sleeping bear. During the construction of the Churchill Falls hydro-electric project in

A black bear awakens to prowl for food in winter. Labrador bears sleep a great deal in winter, but do not hibernate through the season.

central Labrador, one black bear found a disused culvert tile and snuggled down underneath it. The tile was close to the road, where trucks roared past every day. Nevertheless the bear slept for weeks, oblivious of the heavy traffic.

Bears are bold, smart and lazy, and so they are frequently seen around human settlements. Man and his detritus seem to attract them. They love garbage dumps, and sometimes they don't wait until the garbage gets that far. This fondness for refuse once brought a black bear as close to me as I ever want to be: less than a quarter of an inch. Fortunately, there was a pane of glass between us.

I had heard something rummaging through the garbage at the back of the camp where I was staying on the Churchill River, and I peered through the window into the night to determine the cause of the commotion. I am glad I did so before venturing outside, because I found myself looking into the beady brown eyes of a black bear. Its nose was pressed against the outside of the window pane and my nose was pressed against the inside.

I had been taught as a child that bears are as frightened of you as you are of them; but I had no intention of testing that theory. In fact, bears have been known to maul or kill when they are injured, or when a mother bear senses danger to her cubs. You can never tell when a bear is in an ugly mood. I can recall, as a youngster, seeing a black bear sitting on second base in the ball park of my home town of Schreiber, Ontario. The game my friends and I had planned to play was hastily "called on account of bear", until the beast got up and lumbered away.

While bears disappear from Labrador landscapes in the winter, moose can still be seen. Because of their uncommon height—some grow to more than six feet at the shoulder—moose feed during autumn on foliage high in the trees. In winter they face a problem as snow engulfs the trees. Then a herd of moose will gather to trample down the snow in a large area, known as a "moose yard", uncovering enough grass, weeds and seeds to survive until spring.

Although moose will rarely attack a man, they can nevertheless be a menace. Moose like to travel on roads, whenever they can find one. And while they can move at considerable speed once they get under way, they are not very agile when you suddenly come upon them in a speeding car. A full-grown specimen can demolish a big vehicle. The moose generally move down the middle of a road, and they are so high off the ground that they are difficult to see, especially at night, because the trunks of their bodies are higher than a car's headlights. A car will take

A moose takes its ease in a Labrador meadow. The animal, not native to Labrador, was first brought over from Newfoundland by the provincial government in the 1940s but, for no apparent reason, died out. A few years later Canadian moose mysteriously appeared in Labrador; they had moved north of their own volition. In the years since, they have expanded their range as far north as Goose Bay.

the legs out from under a moose so that its body will lift and crash through the windscreen and on to the front seat. I once knew a man who was killed that way.

One early morning on the Churchill River I spotted two handsome cow moose standing in a meadow. It was the rutting season, in early autumn, and they seemed to be on the lookout for males. Cow moose are quite forward in such matters. They emit a low but resonant moan guaranteed to stir the passions of every bull within earshot.

When two or more bulls converge on these beckoning cows, the battle that follows is of epic proportions. I once came upon impressive evidence of such a contest in a forest in western Labrador. The devastation was immense. Throughout a large clearing branches had been ripped off the big trees and the willow, and bushes had been trampled into the ground. The moss had been churned up and the earth and leaves were spattered with blood. I could picture the two bulls charging through the thicket towards each other, their huge heads down, snorting, pawing the ground, and finally colliding like locomotives. A hefty bull moose weighs more than half a ton. Warring bulls like these have been known to lock antlers and, unable to separate, struggle until they collapse with exhaustion. Wolves gather during the impasse and, when the moose fall, move in for the kill.

Moose are found in southern Labrador, but not in the north. The remarkable thing is that they weren't in Labrador at all until a few years ago. Only recently did Canadian moose move up from Quebec province, rapidly expanding their habitat north to establish a firm and apparently permanent base in Labrador.

A similar phenomenon has been the gradual movement of many thousands of the fascinating creatures known as barren land caribou from one area of Labrador to another. Caribou migrate seasonally, but the southern limit of their migration in the west-central region of Labrador is now a hundred miles farther north than it was 20 years ago. Furthermore, their main migration routes have moved east as well as north. A few years ago the migration southwards of the main Labrador herd in November took them each year through the interior of the country. Now they have swung east, towards the Atlantic coast. They even move right through the coastal village of Nain, over the surrounding steep hills and across Nain's ice-filled harbour. Locals still recall with laughter the sight of "Joe, the bush pilot" running across the ice in the harbour just ahead of one onrushing herd to take shelter in his plane. The caribou avoided the plane, but obviously they would not have avoided Joe if they had caught up with him beforehand.

One Nain resident, Tom Osmond, still marvels at the spectacle of a huge herd going through the village. "I put a flashlight on them out the back door," he recalls, "and they just kept going by for hours and hours. I stood there for, it must have been, three hours and watched them, thousands of them. Their eyes reflected the flashlight like Christmas tree bulbs. They were still moving by when I went to bed." That herd, conservatively estimated at more than 30,000, continued pouring in waves over the hills around Nain for the better part of three days and four nights.

Wolves follow caribou migrations, but are more cautious of men. On this occasion the wolves took a detour around the village. They also find their prey difficult to follow because the caribou will let nothing get in their way; a herd will clamber up high hills and swim fast-flowing rivers, and can travel easily over deep snow and spongy muskeg on broad-splayed hoofs especially adapted for the purpose. One advantage the wolves have is that the caribou move so fast and cover such long distances that they leave many of the weak, crippled and young behind. Moreover, the same wolves do not follow a caribou herd throughout its migration; wolves are territorial. So an exhausted caribou can become easy prey to a fresh pack that has just taken up its trail.

It is quite a sight to observe a caribou migration forming up. The animals scatter into small bands on their winter grounds; then, in the spring, they congregate in herds for the trek north. Flying over central Labrador near Esker one fair April morning, I spotted a pair of caribou running out of the thick woods near a frozen pond. As soon as I gained a clear view over the next hill, I could see the reason. A herd was gathering in a valley, moving slowly, and other little groups of stragglers were coming in over the hills to join up, beginning an odyssey that would take them 200 miles to their summer grounds.

On an autumn day I saw another type of migration at its start—this time a flock of birds. I was on the deck of a fishing boat off the northern Labrador coast. Three or four Canada geese appeared in the sky high above the sea, flying purposefully and honking loudly. From a near-by island rose three or four other geese, then two or three more from another island. More and more came up from the islands, swiftly gaining altitude to take their places at the nearest end of the long, high-flying line. The line wavered to and fro, then shaped itself into the characteris-

A caribou lopes across a stream near Ramah, in northern Labrador. Caribou migrate, and in recent years the pattern of movement has unaccountably moved eastwards and northwards; the southern limit is now about a hundred miles north of what it was two decades ago.

tic V formation, and finally disappeared over the horizon to the south.

As I watched them disappear, I recalled a time some years earlier when I was visiting a stretch of beach on the Outer Banks of North Carolina, 2,500 miles south of Labrador. It was November, and I was watching some Canada geese on the last leg of their journey to their winter home in the marshes not much farther south of where I was. As they passed, they were still flying in tight formation and honking lustily, as if they had lost no strength at all on their exhausting journey. But when I walked a little farther down the beach, I came across something black and broken lying in the sand. It was a dead goose—not shot but evidently dead of exhaustion. It seemed such a waste to have come all that way to die.

I have always puzzled over what impels the birds to go on these long migratory flights. Labrador encourages one's interest in the reasons behind all such mass movements because migrations play such a large role in the country's life. The most believable theory I have heard is that the birds originated in the north and lived there all the year round until they were driven south by the Ice Ages. When they were able to return after the great thaw, they developed the habit in winter of going back to their temporary homes in the south and the warmer weather there. This theory, however, does not explain why the Arctic tern nests in the Arctic in summer and winters in the Antarctic, making the annual round trip of some 22,000 miles. (One suggestion is that they dislike darkness.) Or why, of more than one hundred species of warblers in the boreal forest, some migrate much farther south than others.

Do congenial circumstances, such as ample food and a scarcity of predators, weaken the migratory instinct? In the case of the less venturesome warblers it would seem so. The urge to migrate can also be thwarted with no ill effects; the ouananiche is a landlocked version of the migrating salmon and survives in the inland lakes of Labrador that were created by glacial or other geological upheavals thousands of years ago. And yet, if some members of the salmon family can live in fresh water without ever going to sea, others cannot live at sea without returning to fresh water. That is the case of the Atlantic salmon, which has the most magnificent migration story of all.

I became interested in the Atlantic salmon's migratory habits one time a few years ago when I was in Sept Isles, on the Quebec portion of the Labrador Peninsula. The water in the near-by Moisie River had been low that year because of a protracted dry spell, and the salmon coming

Hovering over the water of Labrador's coast, an Arctic tern watches for fish. These hardy little birds have one of the longest migration patterns of any creature; they summer at the edge of the Arctic, in Labrador, and winter in the Antarctic, making a round trip of as much as 22,000 miles every year.

up from the Gulf of St. Lawrence were being grounded in the shallow stretches near the river's mouth. So officials of the Quebec North Shore and Labrador Railway ordered a train of ore cars to be filled with water, and a crew of volunteers netted as many of the stranded fish as they could. A company helicopter picked up the nets and dumped the fish into the water-filled gondola cars. The train carried the salmon about 80 miles upstream, climbing a thousand-odd feet past several steep waterfalls that would have thwarted the exhausted salmon. The fish were then dumped back into the river, and they had a reasonably trouble-free journey the rest of the way to their ancestral spawning grounds on the Labrador Plateau.

The incident appealed to my journalistic sense of the unusual—and to my sense of justice. It was one of the all-too-rare occasions in which man has done anything good for the Atlantic salmon. Man—with his dams, his defoliation, his poisonous effluents and his ruthless over-fishing—has been destroying this magnificent creature for centuries, during which the salmon in countless rivers, including the Thames, the Rhine and the Hudson, have sickened and died.

The salmon's predicament, of course, is its need to spawn at its own birthplace. As each river has been blocked or polluted, the salmon population has been reduced by more or less the number that belonged to that river—and all their potential offspring.

In the days before the "fish lift" on the Moisie that summer, the salmon had been fighting their way over patches of river containing no more than six inches of water. At such times their backs were completely out of the water; only their heads were immersed. They rolled over the round, dry rocks, from one puddle to another, to advance upstream just a few feet at a time. The only way they could rest was by crowding into a few shallow pools, where many became grounded and died. Black bears congregated on the river banks and had a field-day scooping fish out of these teeming traps. Since the salmon, only a few days returned from the open sea, weighed as much as 30 pounds, they provided a glorious feast not only for the bears but also for the smaller animals and birds that ate up what the bears left.

The surviving salmon flipped and flopped ever upstream to the sparse catchments under the rapids and waterfalls. The water in these pools was too low for the fish to get a run at the steep rapids; but they threw themselves at its jagged slope again and again, only to fall back exhausted, with long, bleeding gashes down their sides. Some killed themselves in these efforts; some leaped repeatedly until they gained a ledge; they would pause, and then hurl themselves up the next step. When, by a supreme feat of determination, an occasional salmon reached the top, it found itself once more in a miserable puddle, with nothing but more puddles among the bare rocks ahead. Yet none turned back to the plentiful salt water behind.

It was this impulse to return to its spawning grounds that gave the Atlantic salmon its scientific name. The Roman legionnaires who occupied Gaul and Ancient Britain in the First Century A.D. were treated to a spectacle they had never seen in their native country: that of salmon coming in from the Atlantic and exploding out of the rivers, like silver spears, to leap the waterfalls. Like everyone since then, the Romans were thrilled at the sight of a fish pitting its strength and speed and skill against the terrain and the onrushing waters, getting swept back by the current but always turning and taking another run, gaining a speed of up to 20 m.p.h. before the feel of the current told it to lift off. The Romans called this flashing creature *salar*: the jumper. As a member of a family of fish called the *Salmonidae*, the Atlantic salmon is known to modern ichthyologists as *Salmo salar*.

The salmon has been called the king of fish by no less an authority than Isaak Walton. "He is ever bred in fresh water and never grows big but in the sea," Walton wrote in *The Compleat Angler*. "He has, like many persons of honour and riches which have both their winter and summer houses, his fresh water for summer and salt water for winter to spend his life in." This is a euphemistic way of saying that the salmon is an anadromous fish, bound by its nature to breed in fresh water although it spends about half its life in salt water. What causes this odd behaviour? The best scientific explanation is that its ancestors once lived all year in fresh water and somehow extended their range into salt water. Whatever the reason, fresh water exerts an overwhelming pull on the Atlantic salmon.

On one occasion I was fishing a river so close to its mouth at the ocean that I could see the salmon entering. Or rather, I could see them jumping when they got a hundred yards or so upstream. They kept jumping and jumping, and I found myself wondering fancifully if it was out of elation from having reached fresh water, or if they were practising for the rapids and waterfalls ahead of them. It probably had something to do with the change from salt to fresh water. I've been told that salmon don't go right up the river at first: they swim a little upriver and then out into the brackish water of the estuary again several times to acclimatize themselves.

In Labrador's rivers, as elsewhere, the Atlantic salmon returns from the ocean and compulsively fights its way back, over every obstacle, to its birthplace in the headwaters of the river before laying the eggs of the next generation.

One thing I knew was that they weren't jumping for flies, because one of the differences between salmon and most other migrating fish is that at this point food does not concern them. As a general rule, a migrating salmon eats nothing once it reaches fresh water, and loses weight accordingly. When a salmon snaps at an angler's fly, it is reacting the way I do when I swat a fly. The fly annoys it as the fly annoys me.

None of those lovely, flashing, vaulting creatures swatted at my flies that day, so I presented no obstacle to their ascent towards their breeding grounds a hundred miles or so inland. There, in their own good time, a male and female would come together on a sand or gravel bar at, or very close to, the spot where both had been born. When they are ready to spawn, the male hovers on guard against trout and other intruders while the female lies on one side and uses her tail like a shovel to fashion a nest, called a "redd", in a foot or more of gravel. She settles over the redd and expels her round, orange eggs, then makes way for the male; he instantly covers them with his whitish milt. Often, small trout will brave a snap of the male's powerful hooked jaw to dart in and eat a few of the eggs. Meanwhile, the female scrapes up more gravel just upstream, so it will drift down with the current and cover the eggs. This ritual is repeated once a day for several days until the female has laid about 850 eggs for every pound of her weight. The parents then depart, leaving the buried eggs safe from predators.

Few of the parents make it safely back to the sea. Most are so exhausted that they die on the spawning grounds, and the river current flushes the dead fish downstream along with those still barely alive. The appearance of the latter is nothing short of ghastly. If the dead were not belly up, it would be hard to tell them from the living. The returning fish are called "black salmon": the females are a bluish-black, the males red, black and yellow—like one, long terrible bruise—in striking contrast to the silver leapers that went upriver in the spring.

The few that make it back to sea, however, soon restore themselves. Some live on to make the round trip more than three times. Labrador salmon survive the ordeal more frequently than their counterparts in Canadian rivers farther south. possibly because they come from colder, less polluted water, and their flesh is firmer and better able to withstand the post-spawning deterioration.

The embryos left behind on the spawning grounds by the black salmon are in a hardly less precarious situation than their parents. In a dry winter, with low water, the redd may freeze. A sudden thaw can cause freshets that sweep it away. But if all goes well, two black eyes appear in each egg after about a month. If the eggs survive the spring thaw, they develop into transparent orange creatures, about three-quarters-of-an-inch long, called "alevins". They are provided with a balanced diet by their own yolk sacs for the several weeks until they become free-swimming small fry. Shellfish, eels, trout, ducks and king-fishers take an enormous toll among the alevins. In a hatch of 9,000 eggs, only about 50 succeed in growing into the small fish called "parr". A parr feeds voraciously on floating microscopic life: larvae, worms and insects—and is often mistaken for little trout (by me, for one). In the cold waters of northern Labrador, where all fish grow slowly, a parr may remain in the river for five years, assuming it survives that long. As it grows larger, heron, otter and bear join the list of its predators. Of the 50 parr that emerge from a hatch of 9,000, about four can be expected to reach maturity.

Finally the surviving parr undergo a metamorphosis. They lose their trout-like bars and spots; their tails lengthen and become more deeply forked. They exude an oily chemical called guanin, which turns their sides silver. The "smolt", as they are now called, go downriver and enter the ocean, where their new coloration affords a degree of camouflage. They need it. Among a fresh set of predators at sea are dogfish, thresher and basking sharks, porpoises, seals and killer whales. Dodging these enemies, and meantime gorging on capelin, herring, sprats, shrimp and sand eels, the smolt head out to sea.

Some are content to stay along the coast of Labrador, but not all of them do. Where the latter go has always been one of the great mysteries of fish migration. In the 1960s, however, larger than usual numbers of Atlantic salmon were found along the coast of Greenland; many of them had been tagged previously in Labrador rivers. But whether they had temporarily abandoned their unknown feeding grounds for Greenland waters is a mystery still.

Once the Atlantic salmon were discovered off Greenland, fishing vessels from Denmark arrived to take huge hauls of them. Spurred by high prices in Europe, they increased their annual catch from 50 metric tons to 2,050 metric tons within six years. Under intense international pressure, the Danes have since agreed to exercise some restraint in their catches, lest the Atlantic salmon be exterminated entirely.

Salmon that avoid the fishermen's nets grow to between three and seven pounds during their first year in the ocean. Some precocious one-year-olds return to their rivers to spawn, but most remain at sea to mature for another year or two. As they become full-grown salmon, they change in shape as well as size, filling out along the length of their bodies, their heads becoming proportionately smaller, their tails squarer. And they begin to feel the urge to go home and reproduce.

The salmon born in the rivers of Labrador tend to follow the coast on their homeward journeys. As they swim in and out of the fjords and bays, some peel off from the main body and head up their native rivers. This zigzag mode of travel lends weight to the theory that their uncanny ability to find their way home is governed by the "imprint" of the waters that was instilled in them as small fry. As one Labrador fisherman succinctly explained it to me: "They follows their noses. Them things can smell, you know."

According to ichthyologists, what the salmon smell is the unique chemical combination of the water of their home stream: the minerals in the bed, the vegetation, the character of the water. That they somehow know the water they were reared in has been established by experiments in taking eggs from one stream and hatching them in another. As adults, the fish returned to the stream where they had hatched, not to the one where their eggs had originally been laid.

What has not been so easy to explain is how a salmon under the ice of Davis Strait of Greenland knows that it comes from Labrador or Nova Scotia, or Britain or Spain, and moreover knows how to get back there. Salmon are believed to navigate in the high seas by the moon and stars, by submarine topographical features, by sensing electrical fields, and by the taste and feel of currents. Still, this theory offers no satisfactory explanation of why a salmon will start in the right direction from a thousand miles away.

The people of coastal Labrador are not too interested in such scientific speculation. To them the salmon is an age-old staff of life, one of nature's gifts. They know its ways well enough to be able to catch it, and they do not question its mysterious wanderings. Living as they do in a world of regular natural changes according to the seasons, they tend to look on these changes as divinely decreed. But this does not mean that they take nature for granted; they know that man's survival depends on it. Such a basic fact of life, often overlooked in more civilized places, is impossible to ignore in a land such as this.

A Flowering Moment of Glory

Labrador is a land of surprises, and one of its most astonishing aspects is the variety and riotous colour of its flora. Throughout most of the year the countryside is bleak and forbidding. But then, in a brief burst of glory, Labrador erupts in masses of brilliant foliage. The spectacle is all the more striking because it is so short-lived; northern Labrador's growing season can be as short as three weeks. In this moment of sudden beauty, herbs and grasses, hedges and sedges bud, blossom and then mature before becoming dormant for another 10 to 11 months.

Labrador's flora represent remarkable case studies of natural selection and adaptation. Normally maturing plants cannot survive in this climate and Labrador has fewer species than do the warmer areas. There are about 500 flowering species in Arctic East America, compared with nearly 6,000 in more temperate Australia. Many of Labrador's plants can freeze as stiff as wax flowers, then thaw with the next warm spell and continue their growth. Most survive as long as 10 months with their roots encased in ice. Before the last of the snow has gone, they are sending green shoots out of the frigid ground, ready to blossom again.

Their root systems are shallow and wide, especially in the northern areas where permafrost remains below the thin surface soil throughout the year. The brilliance of the flowers is itself an adaptation: because of the scarcity of pollinating insects (black flies and mosquitoes are not pollinators), many flowers are larger and more colourful to attract what pollinators there are.

The leaves of many Labrador plants are thick and leathery. Some fold in on themselves, to present the smallest possible surface area when flayed by cold winds, then open up when the temperature reaches the minimum for photosynthesis ($+43°$F.). Because of the drying effect of the strong winds, many Labrador plants have developed larger water-storing cells in their leaves and stems. Others turn their stomata—the apertures in stems or leaves—away from the wind. Some plants have protective covering over their leaves. And some, in areas where the soil is too thin to provide enough nutriment, have even turned carnivorous: they have developed devices for trapping insects to supplement their meagre diet.

A clump of Arctic cotton grass (Eriophorum scheuchzeri), one of Labrador's prevalent plants, raises its tassels to the breeze. When these cottony tufts turn to seed, Labrador's strong autumn winds will scatter them widely, assuring propagation of this well adapted species.

Nearly Indestructible Mosses and Lichens

Some of Labrador's most attractive plants can best be appreciated on one's hands and knees. The lichens and mosses, not generally known for brilliant hues elsewhere, here provide a kaleidoscope of colour. But they can be fully appreciated only close up, because they are the ground-huggers of Labrador plants, some of them even miniature.

They have to be. Only these hardy perennials, along with a few sedges and grasses, can survive in the nearly barren tundra. They rarely grow more than a few inches above ground. Their root systems spread out through the soil above the permafrost; often the soil is composed of decayed mosses and lichens. These plants in fact take advantage of the permafrost, because it inhibits drainage in a part of Labrador that has little rainfall.

The mosses and lichens can be found throughout Labrador; but in the north they carpet the tundra floor, bunched together for protection from the harsh winds. These tough plants are almost indestructible. They survive colder conditions than the plants to the south. On the tundra the snowfall is usually lighter, and the winds blow away much of what insulating snow there is. In the bitterly cold temperatures the snow is dry, gritty and abrasive. Yet the lichens and mosses snuggle into rock clefts, bogs and hollows, and spring to life with the first warmth of the new season.

CARIBOU MOSS (CLADONIA ALPESTRIS) AND LEAVES OF THE BLUEBERRY (VACCINIUM ULIGINOSUM)

A LICHEN (PARMELIA) CLOSE UP

JUNIPER-LEAF HAIRY-CAP MOSS (POLYTHRICHUM JUNIPERINUM)

A LICHEN-COVERED ROCK SURROUNDED BY MOSS (DREPANOCLADUS UNCINATUS)

BROWN-SPECKLED CRUSTOSE LICHEN (LECANORA)

LINK LICHEN (XANTHORIA ELEGANS)

BRICK-TOPPED MUSHROOM (HYPHOLOMA)

TWO LICHENS (CLADONIA): CUPPED VARIETY AND RED-TOPPED BRITISH SOLDIER

The Hardy Herbs and Grasses

Along southern Labrador's sandy beaches, clumps of beach grass bind the sand and build dunes, just as they do along sandy shores in other parts of the world. Many of Labrador's grasses employ this same principle of survival in the region's interior areas as well.

A characteristic example is cotton grass. It starts in a clump, which keeps the soil from blowing away. Gradually the clump enlarges as more grass sprouts. Over the years it builds on the organic remains of previous growth, until a firm, spreading tussock has formed (*far right*). Meanwhile, other clumps emerge and grow around it.

The grasses and herbs of Labrador's meadows have adapted to the extremes of climate much as the area's other plants have. They possess shallow, spreading root systems. Their stems are short and often creep along the ground; some stems remain underground. Their leaves are long and narrow, which enables them to resist the drying effect of the wind. Some of the grasses are just thin spikes.

These hardy herbs and grasses are quick to use all the natural help they can get. They form prolific colonies on south-facing slopes, nurtured by the sun and by the spring runoff of melted water from the snow. And they raise their seed-topped heads high so that Labrador's gusty winds will propagate their species far and wide.

A SPIKY HERB MISNAMED STIFF CLUB-MOSS (LYCOPODIUM ANNOTINUM)

SILVERY CANADA REED-GRASS (CALAMAGROSTIS CANADIENSIS)

A CLUMP OF COTTON GRASS (ERIOPHORUM SCHEUCHZERI)

CLUSTERED BERRIES OF THE CRANBERRY-TREE (VIBURNUM EDULE)

FLOWERING ALPINE ARNICA (ARNICA ALPINA)

A Rich Display of Flowers and Berries

An apparent contradiction of Labrador's flora is that the plants most likely to be devoured by bird and beast are the ones most likely to survive. Many of Labrador's shrubs propagate by growing tasty berries that attract hungry birds or animals. The seeds in the berries are thereupon transported abroad in the birds' and animals' stomachs, to be simultaneously sown and fertilized when they are excreted.

Labrador's berry bushes and flowering shrubs are also attractive to the eye; they provide some of the countryside's richest colours. In springtime the flowering shrubs paint the hillsides and meadowlands with splashes of brilliance. In autumn the land is aglow with raspberries and blueberries, curlewberries and cranberries, bakeappleberries and bunch-berries. At the same time, the bushes and shrubs make it difficult for the woodsman to enjoy their display; in some areas of the south the shrubs are almost impenetrable.

As in other parts of the world, many of the berry bushes offer a double feature: flowers in spring and fruits in autumn. But in Labrador the growing season is so truncated that often one can see both features at once. In midsummer a bush will simultaneously display spring flowers that have scarcely begun to fade and autumn fruits that are already starting to make their appearance.

BLUEBERRY (VACCINIUM ULIGNOSUM) AND MOUNTAIN CRANBERRY (VACCINIUM VITIS-IDAEA)

PURPLE SAXIFRAGE (SAXIFRAGA OPPOSITIFOLIA) IN A ROCK CLEFT

BLACK CROWBERRY (EMPETRUM NIGRUM)

FIREWEED (EPILOBIUM ANGUSTIFOLIUM)

ARCTIC POPPY (PAPAVER RADICATUM)

BAKEAPPLE-BERRY (RUBUS CHAMAEMORUS)

ROSEROOT (SEDUM ROSEUM)

FOREGROUND: BIRCHES (BETULA) IN THEIR AUTUMN COLOURS

The Trees' Battle For Survival

Labrador's largest and most conspicuous flora—its trees—flourish only in half the country. There are few above the 55th Parallel and none above the 56th. The southernmost section is thick with forest; but as one goes north the less hardy trees disappear. The maple has succumbed entirely to the harsh climate, so that in Labrador's middle region the autumn colours (left) are more delicate than in lower Canada, the flaming red maple leaves being absent.

The punishing environment has selected out all but about 10 species of trees. Some scarcely resemble their southern relatives. The willow is more bush than tree, and the alder resembles a weed.

The great survivor is the black spruce; it comprises nearly 90 per cent of Labrador's trees. The spruce has shallow roots that can gather sustenance even in areas of permafrost. It can hug the ground (next page). And it is the last of the trees where the forest merges into the tundra.

There, a few other species, stunted by the elements, still fight for their existence. A balsam fir has been found measuring 13 inches in height and 2 inches in diameter—with an age of 54 years. But north of the tree line only the hardiest little plants survive to have their brief bursts of growth during the few bittersweet days interrupting the long winter of the tundra.

SPRUCE (PICEA) ARE REVEALED AS BIRCHES (BETULA) LOSE THEIR LEAVES ON AN AUTUMN HILLSIDE

A SPREADING BRANCH OF A LARCH (LARIX LARICINA)

LABRADOR'S RESILIENT BLACK SPRUCE (PICEA MARIANA)

3/ An Ill-Fated Expedition

Something hidden. Go and find it. Go and look
Behind the Ranges—
Something lost behind the Ranges. Lost and waiting
For you. Go!   RUDYARD KIPLING/ *THE EXPLORER*

The terrain is rumpled and jumbled up as if someone had spilled a bag of laundry. The forest has wrapped itself around the strange whorls and curlicues of rock like a paisley pattern gone mad. Water seems to be everywhere: lakes of all sizes, small round ponds, broad rivers winding through steep valleys, enormous ugly brown-and-yellow bogs and little creeks whose zigs and zags nearly meet. Looking down from a low-flying plane, I see Labrador's interior as its explorers never saw it. Studying its tangled vastness, I wonder: if they could have seen it from up here first, would they ever have started out?

Joe, the pilot, slips off one earphone and shouts something over the roar of the engine. I lean across to him and he points down to our left: "See that river over there? The narrow one? That's the Susan." It is difficult to pick out the river among all the streams running into Grand Lake, but with the help of Joe's large-scale survey map I am finally able to identify it. The Susan: scene of one of the cruellest chapters in the history of Labrador's exploration.

Labrador was one of the last areas on earth to be explored in detail. The first visitors from the Old World briefly touched on its coast and sailed away again. The Norseman Biarni Heriulfson (see Chapter 1), who took a look at the coast in A.D. 986 and called it "worthless country", was followed by other seafaring explorers who spent little more time there. One Norseman who was favourably impressed was

Thorfinn Karlsevni, whose expedition included his wife Gudrid the Fair, 250 men and assorted livestock. They sailed along Labrador's coast in A.D. 1010, and the sagas recount that they marvelled at "the great forests and many wild animals" and the beaches they called "wonderstrands" Still, they appear to have settled in Newfoundland, to the south-east.

An exploration in the 15th Century gave the area its name, but evidently it was a case of mistaken identity. In 1499, Joao Fernandez, a *lavrador*, or husbandman, of the Azores, was granted letters-patent from Portugal's King Manuel to search for islands in the New World. In the summer of 1500, Fernandez sighted land and decided to call it *Tierra del Lavrador*, Land of the Husbandmen. Apparently what he had seen was Greenland, and it was a century later before the name was shifted to its present area.

This rugged coastline briefly intrigued the famous French explorer Jacques Cartier, who sailed by it on the way to his discovery of southern Canada in 1534. But Cartier, too, lost interest. It was, he wrote, a land "of stones and rocks, frightful and ill-shaped, for in all the said north coast I did not find a cartload of earth though I landed in many places. . . . In short, I deem . . . that it is the land God gave to Cain".

During the centuries when the rest of the Americas were being opened up by explorers, fur traders and treasure-seekers, the interior of Labrador remained a mystery to all except some roving bands of Naskaupi and Montagnais Indians and a handful of "Liveyeres" (*live-heres*—indigenous people) of mixed white, Indian and Eskimo blood. They lived by hunting, trapping and fishing; and they followed well-established routes from which they rarely strayed. They also resented intruders. John Christian Erhardt, the first Moravian missionary to visit Labrador, was murdered by the Eskimos he tried to convert.

Even the intrepid Captain James Cook, charting the Labrador coast between 1763 and 1767, found it so uninviting that he avoided going ashore. Another surveyor was Lieutenant Roger Curtis, R.N. When he charted a stretch of Labrador's coast in 1772 and 1773, he recorded, with good reason, that there was no part of the British dominions so little known as Labrador; his journal is littered with such phrases as "frightful mountains", "unfruitful valleys", and "blighted shrubs".

The American travel writer Henry Youle Hind explored Labrador in 1861, and published an account in which he declared that "words fail to describe the appalling desolation of the Labrador tableland". A particularly poignant account was left by four students from Bowdoin College, of Brunswick, Maine, who went up the Grand (now Churchill)

River in 1891. Their canoe overturned in the Horseshoe Rapids. Their gear had been improperly stowed and they lost about a quarter of their food supplies, plus cooking utensils, a shotgun and a revolver. They reached their destination of Grand Falls, but on their return they lost almost all their remaining equipment and provisions when a campfire they had failed to extinguish turned into a minor forest fire and wiped out their camp. But they made up in pluck what they lacked in expertise. When they finally staggered to the safety of a trapper's cabin—ragged, shoeless and starving—they mustered enough strength for a rousing Bowdoin College yell.

College students and missionaries, seasoned explorers and surveyors —Labrador challenged and repelled them. By the turn of the 20th Century, after an age of exploration by such men as Sir Richard Burton, David Livingstone and Henry Stanley, the jungles of Africa had been mapped and many of the Himalayas had been climbed. Yet Labrador remained mainly unexplored. At that point a 29-year-old nature writer in New York decided to remedy the situation.

His name was Leonidas Hubbard, Jr. He was a product of the America of his time, a "manly" man, an admirer of Teddy Roosevelt, whom he physically resembled, and from whom he borrowed his favourite superlative: "bully". Son of a pioneer farmer in Michigan, Hubbard was a contributor to such popular magazines as the *Saturday Evening Post* and the *Atlantic Monthly*, and assistant editor of the New York-based outdoors magazine *Outing*. He had taken two lengthy trips in the Canadian bush, one in northern Quebec and one off Lake Superior's North Shore; but he could scarcely qualify as an experienced explorer, as his adventure was about to prove.

Hubbard had become fascinated with Labrador. He pinned a map of the peninsula on the wall of his study in Congers, N.Y. In the safety of his home, beside the hearth on which he liked to broil bacon as if over a campfire, Hubbard concocted a scheme to trek through a part of central Labrador that even most of the Indians had avoided. His dream was to map this unexplored area; on his return he hoped to write magazine articles and a book that would make him famous. It was still an age that glorified explorers.

Early in 1903, Hubbard came into an inheritance that gave him the wherewithal to launch his expedition. He outlined his plan to Dillon Wallace, an affluent young New York lawyer and amateur outdoorsman who had accompanied Hubbard on camping trips in Upper New York

State. Sitting by the fire on one of their outings, Hubbard described his proposition. "Think of it, Wallace," he said. "A great unknown land right near home, as wild and primitive today as it has always been! I want to see it. I want to get into a really wild country and have some of the experiences of the old fellows who explored and opened up the country where we are now."

Wallace also felt this call. The two men had other traits in common: a strong religious bent, a disdain for "quitters", and a penchant for quoting Kipling, especially a poem entitled "The Explorer":

> Till a voice, as bad as Conscience, rang interminable
> Changes
> On one everlasting Whisper day and night repeated—so:
> "Something hidden. Go and find it. Go and look
> "Behind the Ranges—
> "Something lost behind the Ranges. Lost and waiting
>   "For you. Go!"

"It's a big thing, Wallace," said Hubbard. "It ought to make my reputation."

Hubbard persuaded his friend to come with him. He traced for Wallace the proposed route on the map on his study wall. They would go north-west from Grand Lake up the Naskaupi River, thence to the North West River and its headwaters at Lake Michikamau, at the time the largest lake in eastern Labrador. (Lake Michikamau is now part of Smallwood Reservoir—see map pp. 18-19.) The overland distance for this part of their journey would have measured about 200 miles, but it would be inestimably longer by the river route. They would then cross Lake Michikamau from end to end, a passage of some 80 miles, to the point where it joined the George River. Right there, at the junction of the Michikamau and the George, Hubbard hoped to make contact with the Naskaupi Indians and gather material for an article on their primitive existence; he expected to get there by late August or early September, so that he could participate in the Indians' annual caribou hunt.

Thereafter Hubbard proposed to follow one of three courses, depending on the circumstances. Either route, Hubbard was convinced, would take them through uncharted areas, which they could map and about which they could write on their return. If they failed to meet with the Indians where the Michikamau and the George joined, they would go north on the George for about 300 miles, to the Hudson's Bay Post on Ungava Bay. If they did not meet the Naskaupi, Hubbard thought he might purchase snowshoes and a dog team, and trek across the

At the Hudson's Bay trading post that served as the jumping-off place for their expedition, Leonidas Hubbard, Jr. (left) and Dillon Wallace looked confidently at the camera brought along to record their odyssey. The remarkable photographs on the following pages, taken by the explorers themselves, were published in Wallace's book describing the expedition. The photographs on page 96 were taken by Mrs. Hubbard's companions on her expedition.

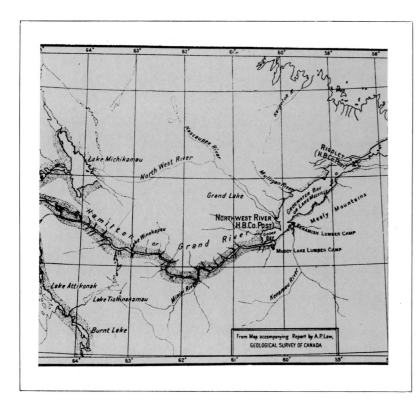

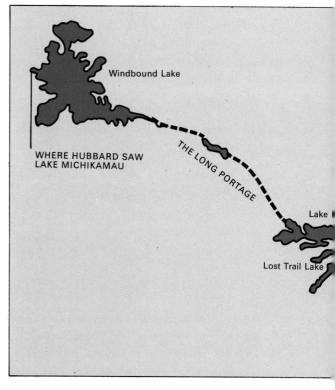

Labrador Plateau to the St. Lawrence River. The third option was to backtrack down the North West-Naskaupi river system to Grand Lake, thence to Hamilton Inlet and to the east coast (see map above).

It was an uncertain scheme to begin with. To make matters worse, the map on which Hubbard was basing all his plans was incorrect. A Canadian Geological Survey map, it had been prepared by a geologist named A. P. Low, who had sketched in a river called the North West, connecting with the Naskaupi about 25 miles north of Grand Lake. (Low had carefully noted in his report that he had not personally surveyed the river; the Montagnais Indians had told him it was there.) Hubbard intended to trace the North West to Lake Michikamau. The trouble was that there was no such river in the area.

Complicating the situation even more, there *was* a North West River nearly a hundred miles south of the area indicated by Low's map. Hubbard did know about this one, however, because there was a Hudson's Bay Company station on its bank. Called the North West River Post, the station was a logical starting point for the expedition.

The major fallacy in Hubbard's plan stemmed from this 1896 map (left) by the surveyor A. P. Low. The plan included traversing a North West River; but there was no such river in this area. The map on the right traces the actual route of the expedition from its start (lower right) through many wrong turns to an agonizingly close approach (upper left) to the original goal, Lake Michikamau. Hubbard, Wallace and Elson returned along the same route, Hubbard collapsing on the way back. Elson went on to find a rescue party that saved Wallace, but Hubbard died at the spot indicated at the right of the map.

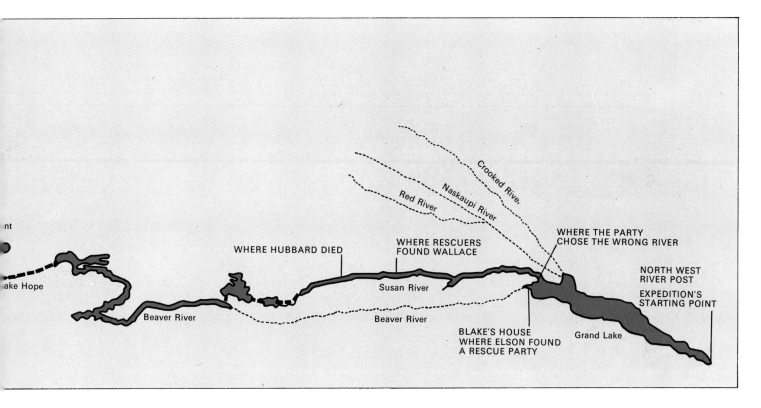

Before setting out, Hubbard enlisted the services of a third adventurer. He was a burly Scots-Cree hunter from the James Bay region of Ontario, named George Elson. Elson was an able woodsman, but he had never been in Labrador. Nevertheless, he was to serve as chief guide.

The expedition did not get under way auspiciously. The steamship that carried the three men from St. John's, Newfoundland, to the Labrador coast took four days longer than scheduled. While moving down Hamilton Inlet towards the North West River Post they were stranded on an island by bad weather. It was July 11, 1903, nearly a month after their departure from New York, before they reached the North West River Post. And there they found that their enthusiasm for the expedition was not shared by the local trappers. Hubbard had hoped that at least one Labrador trapper could accompany them. But none of them was interested. The trappers gave the strangers what information they could, and warned that they would never make it. They watched solemnly as Hubbard, Wallace and Elson set out from the post on the morning of July 15, 1903.

After missing the river Hubbard had aimed for, the explorers found themselves on a stream that dwindled into rapids. They were forced to push their canoe through them and sometimes portage around steep waterfalls.

The three explorers were in a single, 18-foot canoe. It was laden with equipment and provisions, including a camera (see box right), but not enough for three men striking out into the Labrador wilderness for two months or more. They intended to live largely off the land.

On their first day out they explored Grand Lake. On the second day they turned from the lake up a river they thought was the Naskaupi. It was not. Somehow they had passed the mouth of that broad river without noticing it, about three miles before the waterway they chose. This was the Susan River.

From the moment Hubbard, Wallace and Elson steered up the Susan, it proved to be a canoeman's nightmare. They had scarcely paddled a hundred yards when the water became too swift. They tried poling the canoe, but the weight of one man at the stern doing the poling caused the canoe to scrape the bottom. All three had to jump into the water and manhandle it over the rocks. Then they came to stretches where the water was too shallow or strong even for this method. So they had to resort to portaging: carrying the canoe and everything in it overland, hacking their own trails through thick bush and sloppy swamps choked with alders, and clambering over hills and down precipitous valleys.

Their first mistake was soon compounded by another: because Hubbard wanted to lighten the load and feed up for the hard work ahead, they were prodigal with their supplies. They feasted on pancakes with sugar syrup and bacon. It was two days before Wallace voiced his suspicion that they were on the wrong river; a trapper at the Hudson's Bay Post had told them that they could easily paddle up the Naskaupi for 18 or 20 miles, but they had encountered rapids just above the mouth of the Susan. Stubbornly, Hubbard insisted that the trapper must have been confused, so they continued to toil up the wrong river.

Hubbard was anxious to hurry on because of their late start. It was now well past the middle of July, and they were discovering that Labrador's brief summer could be as merciless as its winter. The temperature in the shade climbed to over 90°F. When it was not broiling hot, it was raining. The drenching downpours made the going uncomfortable and the footing slippery in the portages; but the rain at least provided a temporary respite from the scourge of flies. The rest of the time black flies swarmed around them, biting them until they had raw wounds on their exposed hands and wrists, and blood streaming down their faces. At night the mosquitoes stung unremittingly. The fly bites made Wallace sick and his face was so swollen he could hardly see.

Within a week both Wallace and Hubbard were ill—Wallace vomiting and Hubbard suffering from diarrhoea. Hubbard became so weak that they had to halt. Inside their tent the temperature hit 104°F. Hubbard recovered enough to push on—and to make other, more far-reaching miscalculations. He proposed that they abandon larger quantities of their food in order to lighten the load. When George Elson objected, Hubbard compromised by leaving some of the food in caches along the trail, in case they were forced to retreat. They jettisoned their coats because of the heat, regardless of the hardship this would mean in colder weather later on. During one portage Hubbard missed a golden chance for a sustained food supply: he found himself within a hundred feet of a caribou, but he had left his rifle in the canoe.

Throughout, Hubbard remained convinced they were on the Naskaupi River. And all this time he conscientiously kept a diary. His hearty capacity for self-delusion shines through in this entry for July 19:

"Found small rocky stream coming in about a mile up. Suppose it is the Red Wine River. Two miles up to a 2-mile stretch of good water. Best of all a portage route leading in at the foot. We followed this over

KIT FOR A LABRADOR TREK

The equipment and provisions taken by the three-man Hubbard expedition in their 18-foot canoe:

1 WATERPROOF SILK TENT
4 BLANKETS
2 TARPAULINS
3 SETS OF SPARE CLOTHES
2 .45-70 WINCHESTER RIFLES
2 .22 PISTOLS
AMMUNITION
1 CAMERA & FILM
1 SEXTANT & ARTIFICIAL HORIZON
2 COMPASSES
COOKING UTENSILS
120 LB. FLOUR
25 LB. BACON
13 LB. LARD
30 LB. PEAMEAL
8 LB. HARD-TACK BISCUIT
10 LB. MILK POWDER
10 LB. RICE
8 LB. APPLES (DRIED BY HUBBARD'S MOTHER)
2 LB. SALT
30 LB. SUGAR
5 LB. COFFEE
10 LB. TEA

the hill to the Red Wine River, and found old cuttings. This pleases us a heap. It shows that we are on the old Montagnais trail and will probably have their portage routes clear through, and that they probably found lakes and good water farther on, or they would never have fought this bad water. Tomorrow we tackle the 2-mile portage with light hearts. We are three miles south of where Low's map places us. Am beginning to suspect that the Nascaupee River [his spelling of the Naskaupi], which flows through Seal Lake, also comes out of Michikamau, and that Low's map is wrong. Bully stunt if it works out that way." In other words, the map might be wrong, but still Hubbard was convinced that they were on the right track.

It turned out that the easy portage he had anticipated the next day took them through a mile and a half of swamp and over a steep hill. Wallace collapsed at the end of it. The two miles of good canoe water Hubbard had thought he saw actually stretched less than half a mile. Then came another day of portaging. It went on day after day, until the Susan eventually petered out. They had covered only 80 miles in 15 days.

Still, Hubbard firmly believed that they had been on the Naskaupi River. And at this point, where the Susan dwindled to a trickle, they found a creek. Hubbard guessed that this creek might lead them into the North West River. They headed up the creek, but it, too, petered out. From that point they groped overland through swampland, still searching for the North West River shown on Low's map. By now their provisions were alarmingly low. In the small streams they encountered there should have been plenty of trout; but they did not catch enough to supplement their food supplies. They shot a few geese and ducks, but game was generally scarce.

Their earlier improvidence was already exacting its price. They now realized that they should have brought along a shotgun to shoot wild-fowl on the wing; but Hubbard had decided that the necessary number of shells would be too bulky to carry. Hubbard's moccasins broke through at the soles; two of his toenails were torn off, and a wide cut was opened on one of his heels. He patched his wounds with electrician's tape; they had not thought to bring a first-aid kit.

In spite of the back-breaking work on the portages, the horrors of the flies and mosquitoes, the heat by day and chill by night, Hubbard remained sanguine. By campfire he quoted Kipling and kept imagining that he had seen signs of Indian trails. And sure enough, three weeks after the start of their expedition, their luck took a brief turn for the better; they came upon a broad river, deep enough for good canoe travel.

They had stumbled on to the Beaver River, on a disused Indian route that eventually connected with Lake Michikamau. Once on the Beaver, Hubbard started catching more and bigger trout. One day, within a matter of minutes, he hooked 15, averaging more than half a pound each. But the Beaver was no easy passage. They had to make more portages over rugged terrain. It was now August 7. They were 24 days into their trek, and the summer heat was giving way to raw winds and slashing rain. The hard work and the meagre, unbalanced diet provided by their fast-dwindling food supplies had brought them to the first stages of starvation. But then, on August 12, a big bull woodland caribou appeared along the river shore. It took five shots for Hubbard, who was no sharpshooter, to bring the animal down. "Best day of trip!" he exclaimed in his diary. They were in open water. They had found an old Indian trail along the Beaver. They ate roasted caribou steaks for lunch. And they dried a supply of meat to carry along.

Their good luck held as they paddled up the Beaver. On one day Hubbard and Wallace caught 84 big trout within an hour. Elson shot more geese and partridge, and they feasted on them by the campfire. Then the Beaver too came to an end.

They found themselves on a broad lake; characteristically, Hubbard called it Lake Hope. On its shores was evidence that Indians had been there. Hubbard and his companions were sure now that they were on the old Indian trail to Lake Michikamau. They had indeed blundered on to a passable trail. They hoped to pick it up on the other side of the lake.

They crossed Lake Hope on the sunny Sunday of August 23, 1903. They could not pick up the Indian trail, but they paddled through a strait between two high mountains—and broke the silence with three cheers. Before them lay a larger body of water. They were sure that it was one of the bays of Lake Michikamau.

For three days they impatiently explored the area, before they realized finally that they were not on the Michikamau. This lake was much too small. They gave it a well earned name: Lost Trail Lake. But they remained persuaded nonetheless that Lake Michikamau lay in that general direction, and in their impatience they compounded this error, too. Instead of reversing their course and returning to Lake Hope and the Indian trail, they pushed on through the trackless forest in the direction they were convinced would take them to Lake Michikamau.

They did find another lake; but not Lake Michikamau. By now it was August 28, and Labrador's early autumn was upon them. There was a

"Lake Hope" was the name Hubbard gave to this body of water that he believed to be a bay leading to Lake Michikamau. The lake turned out to be misnamed: it had no connection to Lake Michikamau.

A high point of the expedition was the day Hubbard added to their meagre supplies by shooting a caribou. Elson stripped it of everything but the antlers, which he (right) and Wallace held up for Hubbard's camera.

Back-packing the gear and provisions over the long portages was heavy work for the three men. At first Wallace had trouble lifting 75 pounds; but later he found he was able to haul up to 100 pounds (above).

snap in the air. The fish stopped biting. The three men were reduced to living mainly on blueberries, mossberries and wild cranberries, which did not help Hubbard's recurring diarrhoea. They scoured the lake, but finally had to admit there was no outlet that led to Lake Michikamau. They decided to call this one Disappointment Lake. But Hubbard remained undaunted. On they went overland, into the unknown country to the north, still hoping to come to Michikamau.

Carrying their canoe, they ploughed through swamps and stumbled over hills, lashed by wind, rain and sleet. They were growing weaker, and their thin summer clothes were in tatters. But they plunged on, encouraging each other with the bully slogan, "Michikamau or bust". It took them 13 days to cover the 40 miles from Disappointment Lake to another large and promising lake. There Hubbard and Elson climbed a hill and did indeed sight Lake Michikamau less than 10 miles in the distance. The date was September 9.

Excited, Hubbard began making plans to portage over a series of ponds to the lake. Now they knew where they were. Once across Lake Michikamau they would find the George River, and on the George River were the caribou grounds. The caribou would provide them not only with meat but also with skins for parkas, leggings and boots. They would make snowshoes from branches and strips of caribou hide, and then they could set out across the plateau as soon as winter set in and there was a firm snow cover on the ground.

The lake they were on was later well named Windbound Lake. (Along with Lake Michikamau, Windbound Lake has been absorbed in Smallwood Reservoir.) On September 12, Hubbard's diary records high winds and snow showers, making canoe travel impossible. The weather was the same next day and the next. The winds continued and the temperature dropped below freezing. Unable to fish or hunt because of the recurring storms, they spent days huddled in their tent.

Finally, on the night of September 15, as they sat shivering by their campfire, Hubbard said: "Boys, what do you say to turning back?"

They were in sight of their goal. Yet they agreed that they could not reach it. The weather was too much for them in their weakened condition. They could not get to the caribou grounds before the animals migrated south. The safer direction was back along the way they had come. At least they knew that route, and with luck they could find some of the caches of food they had left on the way up.

But for five days the wind blew so hard that they could not go out on to the lake. They had had very little to eat while waiting. Hubbard had caught a few small *nanycush* (Labrador lake trout), which they ate head, entrails and all. They also staved off starvation with tiny portions of their emergency food supply of peameal and flour.

When finally they were able to start their bitter retreat, 16 pounds of peameal and some tea made up all the emergency rations they had left. Their original starting point—the North West River Post—was now their destination; it was about 300 miles away. But Hubbard's hopes remained high. He cheerfully noted in his diary: "When we reach the big river [the Beaver] we can I think nearly live on the fish we get there. From there too, there may be more signs of caribou. About four days more and we ought to reach a remnant of flour we threw away. It was wet and lumpy, but we will welcome it now. It, if it is usable, will see us to the head of Grand Lake where Skipper Tom Blake has a winter hunting shanty. It promises to be a hungry trip, but it is a man's game."

It was a 40-mile portage back to Lake Disappointment, in raw and rainy weather. On the first day they caught four small trout and shot a duckling. On the third day Elson brought down a goose. They saved part of the bird and made a sparse banquet that included the entrails and chunks of fat from the neck; the rest of the goose, along with some fish with their entrails and roe, got them through the next two days. The rain turned to snow and sleet. By the end of September Hubbard was failing badly, weak with hunger and illness, and he took to babbling sentimentally about his wife and mother, and about the food he had once eaten in restaurants in New York City. He could not keep pace with the others on the trail. Wallace also was sick, vomiting frequently.

They were virtually crawling when they reached the Beaver River on October 9. They shot the rapids going downriver, taking chances they ordinarily would not have taken. The fish were driven to the bottom by the frigid water and stopped biting. When the men's supplies from their last catch of fish ran out, they started eating the boiled strips of caribou hide they had been carrying ever since Hubbard's kill. They did find one bag of the flour they had discarded on their way north. The contents were rotten, but they were able to salvage little lumps of mouldy flour, which they ate with strips of caribou hide.

It was here that Hubbard made his final, tragic decision. He decided to depart from the broad Beaver River and cross on foot through the valley of the Susan. That was the way they had come, he reasoned, so there was less chance of getting lost on the way back. Elson disagreed; he held to the woodsman's axiom: "When in trouble, stick to your canoe." He was right, though for a reason he could not know: had they kept to the Beaver River, they would have come out at Grand Lake, about 40 miles from the North West River Post, which was their goal.

Before leaving the Beaver, they came upon the carcass of Hubbard's caribou. Wolves and other scavengers had stripped it to the bones. But the desperate men took the skeleton, the hoofs and the antlers and boiled them all, drinking the broth in spite of the maggots floating in it. Then they struck out for the valley of the Susan, abandoning their canoe.

They backtracked on the route they had taken from the Susan, and were thus able to extract some sustenance from more of the garbage they had left along the trail on the way up: rotting goose heads, the scrapings from an old lard pail, a bit of baking powder sticking to a rusty tin. They reached the valley of the Susan and started down. But on Saturday, October 17, Hubbard stumbled and fell for the last time. His companions put him to bed in the tent.

That night they had a last strategy session. They agreed that Wallace and Elson would go on without Hubbard. Wallace would try to find more of their cast-off provisions and bring them back to Hubbard; the two would wait for Elson to find a rescue party. Next morning, after tearfully kissing Hubbard's cheek, Wallace and Elson stumbled away in a rainstorm. And Hubbard wrote another hopeful entry in his diary: "Alone in camp, estimated (overestimated, I hope) distance from the head of Grand Lake, 33 miles. For two days past we have travelled down our old trail with light packs. We left a lot of flour wet—about 11 miles below here, 12 miles (approximately) below that about a pound of milk powder, 4 miles below that about 4 pounds of lard."

Hubbard let his fire go out, closed the flap of the tent from the inside and waited for rescue or for death.

Wallace and Elson made slow progress. At night they made a smoky fire with rotten trees. Next morning the snow was up to their knees. Elson shot a grouse; they tore it apart and ate it raw.

With his uncanny instinct for locating things in the bush, Elson found another old flour bag. The flour was a mouldy green and black lump. They divided it between them. Wallace kept what he reckoned would sustain him and Hubbard for three days; Elson took the rest for his 25-mile trek to the head of Grand Lake, where he hoped to find the rescue party. Wallace was about 15 miles from Hubbard's tent when he turned back up the valley.

He could hardly see. The smoke of punk fires of the last two nights had all but blinded him. Unable to read his compass, he floundered

On the way back, Hubbard became so exhausted that he stumbled and fell, could not carry his share of the load, and frequently had to rest along the trail (above). Wallace and Elson finally left him in his tent and went on for help.

through the snow. He camped in a spruce grove, making a fire and choking down some of the flour mould mixed with melted snow.

Next day there was a blizzard. Wallace tried to cross the ice on the river and broke through. He pulled himself up on the opposite shore, but his clothes froze stiff, and he could not walk. He built another fire to thaw them out; the thought of Hubbard waiting for him made him frantic. When he started out again, he found that he could not see well enough to travel. Again he was forced to camp.

For two more days he pressed on towards Hubbard as well as he could, keeping himself alive with a gruel made from the flour mould. It nauseated him. Another stiff storm blew up, covering all the landmarks on the trail. But he knew that he must be near the camp by now, and he shouted again and again for Hubbard. Hearing no reply, he continued to reel blindly up the valley through the snow. He had been six days on his 15-mile trek, and he began to worry that he had overshot the camp. He turned back and tried to cross the river, and again plunged through the ice. He had a momentary impulse to let the current carry him under. But he found the will to drag himself out and build another fire.

Now Wallace began to experience all the signs of a person dying of exposure. He wanted to go to sleep forever. But he had hallucinations, one of which took the form of his dead wife urging him to carry on. He rose and wandered back down the valley in a daze; he had lost all sense of time. But he still struggled to stay alive.

Finally he reached the end of his endurance. With the voices of Hubbard, his late wife and his sisters whispering inside his head, he dozed off again, lying in the snow beside a little punk fire.

While Wallace wandered up the valley, Elson staggered down it. His boots were torn to bits and he churned through snow up to his knees, over the rugged, hilly country. Always a good hunter, he shot two porcupines on the first day and four partridges on the third. He went on for a total of five days, in the killing cold and through the snowstorms, over the hills and across the valleys. And at about 10 a.m. on October 26, he reached Grand Lake.

He was unable to find Skipper Blake's cabin. So he set out to make the 40-mile trek around Grand Lake to the Hudson's Bay North West River Post. His progress was blocked by a broad river mouth, split in two by an island. He tried to wade across it, but almost drowned when the cold water made his legs seize up.

He waded ashore, curled up and slept fitfully until next morning, when he tried to get across the river again, with no greater success. He collected some driftwood and tied the pieces together with his pack strap and some fishing line to make a raft. When he launched it, the logs started to separate in the strong current of the river mouth. Elson spread himself over the raft to try to hold the pieces of driftwood together, the water washing over him and nearly drowning him again. Spreadeagled on his raft, he was blown out into the lake. After two hours the wind changed and drove him back close enough to the island in the river mouth so that he could pole himself ashore.

He pushed over some rotten stumps and tied them together into another raft of sorts. By dusk he succeeded in poling himself across to the mainland. There he saw a rowing boat on the shore. His hopes soared. Now he could row down the lake to the North West River Post.

As he approached the boat he heard a noise he could not identify. Then he realized what it was: a baby crying. He stumbled in the direction of the sound and saw a house. A girl appeared in the doorway, took one look at the gaunt, bearded man and screamed. An older woman came to join her. "Don't be scared, ladies, I couldn't hurt a rabbit," Elson croaked. "Ain't there any men here?"

The older woman was the wife of another Blake—Donald Blake, a trapper who had built the little log house during the previous summer. By the time she had fed Elson on partridge stew, bread and butter and molasses—a meal that caused him painful stomach cramps—her husband and his 17-year-old brother Gilbert had come home from gathering wood. They asked Elson what river the party had followed that summer. He said it was the Naskaupi. But when he described it, they told him it was the Susan. George said: "Well I'll be blamed."

Then he asked them, "What river was this one I crossed with the raft?" They said it was the Beaver. If Hubbard had listened to Elson's advice, all three men could have come out on Grand Lake long ago.

Donald and Gilbert Blake started out the same evening to pick up two other trappers—Allen Goudie and Duncan MacLean—at their camp seven miles away, to form a rescue party. The four men set out immediately. Running on their snowshoes where possible, they moved 10 miles up the Susan Valley by nightfall of October 29.

They snowshoed all the next day, firing a rifle at intervals in the hope that they were within hearing distance of Hubbard and Wallace. On the third morning Donald Blake said he smelled smoke. Allen Goudie sniffed the air and the two agreed that there was smoke blowing up the valley. Hurrying back down the trail, they came across a set of tracks.

They followed them, shouting and firing their rifles. They mounted a snowbank and behind it was Wallace, roused from his dying stupor by their shouts. A faint smudge of fire was still glowing; they had smelt it from a mile and a half away.

As they fed Wallace bread and butter and tea, they ascertained that he must have passed them, going down the valley, the previous evening. His trouser legs had been torn off by the brambles, and little was left of the socks that were the only covering on his feet. For a coat he wore a ragged piece of blanket. When he had started out on the expedition, he had weighed 170 pounds; he now weighed about 90. A doctor later told him that the toughening-up process in the bush had saved him. No man who had not been hardened by exposure could have survived what he had endured in that last week.

With Wallace's guidance the rescuers found Hubbard's tent. Hubbard was still inside, wrapped in his blankets. He was dead.

Only a few yards from Hubbard's tent were Wallace's tracks and the remains of one of his fires. He had slept there and blindly staggered away from his destination. No doubt this miscalculation had saved him: the trappers explained to him that, if he had discovered Hubbard's body, he would have settled down to wait—and, like Hubbard, he probably would have died: only his continuing exertions, moving about in the bush, had kept him alive.

As it was, Wallace almost did die in the days that followed, as the poison from his gangrenous frozen feet spread through his system. Only the providential visit of a medical student, who treated him at the North West River Post, saved him from death. Wallace and Elson spent the winter there, then set out in the spring to recover Hubbard's body. They took it to the coast by dog sled. On May 13, 1904, they loaded their sad burden on a steamship, to transport it to New York for burial. The body, in a spruce coffin made by a carpenter at the North West River Post, was frozen solid even then.

I have recounted this story at length because it is probably the most dramatic of all the tales of exploration in Labrador. But it is not any less representative. From Henry Youle Hind to the prospecting parties of today, anyone who has ventured into the Labrador interior has had to face the same challenges as did the Hubbard party.

The Hubbard expedition accomplished practically none of Hubbard's aims. No new maps were made; no rivers or lakes were surveyed; Hubbard did not even succeed in doing his article on the Naskaupi Indians'

The rescue party—four men found by Elson just before he collapsed—were local trappers (left to right): Gilbert Blake, Duncan MacLean, Allen Goudie and Donald Blake. They located Wallace on the point of death, but were too late to save his friend Hubbard.

In early spring a dog team, hauling Hubbard's coffin to the nearest port for shipment home, paused for rest along the snow-covered route. Wallace took Hubbard's body back to New York on the Newfoundland steamer Sylvia.

caribou hunt; and he would never write the book that would make him famous. Wallace did write a book, *The Lure of the Labrador Wild*, to which I am indebted for much of my narrative. His account is full of object lessons of what not to do. Yet the experience did not keep Wallace away from Labrador.

Just a year after his return to civilization, he succumbed to the lure again and set out to map some of the same area. This time his partner was a New York sportsman named Clifford Easton. And this time they were considerably better prepared for Labrador's hazards. Still, they barely escaped with their lives on two occasions—once when their canoe overturned with most of their supplies, and once when the weather pinned them down for a week in a hut with no food.

Wallace's book also provoked an odd expedition to the same area. The expedition's leader was Leonidas Hubbard's widow.

Mrs. Mina Hubbard was an amateur explorer herself, and familiar with the woods, having been born and raised in Ontario. She evidently believed that Wallace had capitalized on her husband's death. She determined to complete Hubbard's mission, and in 1905 she set out on what she called the Second Hubbard Expedition. Although she vehemently defended her husband's methods, she made more thorough

Hubbard's widow, Mina, retraced his route two years later.

Naskaupi women crowded curiously around their visitor.

At Ungava Bay, far north of the point where her husband had had to turn back, his widow made a ceremonious landing.

plans and took greater precautions. For a guide she recruited the young Labrador trapper Gilbert Blake, who had participated in Wallace's rescue. The other members were George Elson, as resourceful as ever, and two canoemen from Elson's home territory on James Bay.

Her equipment included a hiking outfit consisting of a short skirt worn over knickerbockers; a sweater; and a belt holding a revolver, a cartridge pouch and a hunting knife. She also wore knee-length leather boots and a hat on which she could drape fly-netting. Her gear also included a small tent, an air mattress and a hot-water bottle to be filled with water heated over the camp fire.

She succeeded where her husband had failed, braving rapids that elicited the admiring comment from her friend George Elson: "I have seen lots of men who would jump out of the canoe if we tried to take them where you have been just now." Every evening she recorded the day's progress in her own diary. Mice and lemmings ate holes in her hat and her boots. Black flies squirmed through the netting on her hat. She commented that she was glad she had brought no mirror, in which she would have seen the damage the flies did to her face.

Mrs. Hubbard succeeded in mapping the river and lake system between Grand Lake and the Ungava coast. She also proved that the elusive North West River did not exist. She returned safely, to write her own account of a 576-mile journey that took 61 days. Her book recorded not only her explorations but also her appreciation of this wild area. On August 16, she wrote: "My tent was sweet that night with the fragrance of its carpet of balsam boughs, and a big bunch of twin flowers, which grew in profusion there; but it was late before I slept. Perhaps two hours after, I awoke to find a big moon peering into my face through the open front of my tent."

At such times, Mrs. Hubbard could understand the fascination of Labrador that had lured her husband to his death.

NATURE WALK / A Trek Along the River

PHOTOGRAPHS BY ROBERT WALCH

Voisey Bay is a hook-shaped indentation in the northern coast of Labrador about 50 miles south-west of Nain, which is the nearest settlement. In the early part of the 20th Century the bay served as a jumping-off place for some of the explorers of the barren interior of Labrador. I was thinking of these men on a misty morning in mid-July as I started out on a short trek with the photographer Robert Walch and our guide, Horace Goudie, to observe the varied flora and fauna of the Voisey Bay area. In a place such as this the countryside changes little with time, so I reasoned that I would be seeing what the explorers had seen.

Already that morning I had somewhat duplicated the experience of the American explorer William B. Cabot, when he sailed up the bay in 1904. From our motor boat I caught a glimpse of a grampus—a small whale—momentarily breaking the surface to breathe. A grampus is about 12 feet long, but when it comes up to blow, all you can make out is a shiny strip of black back arching gracefully above the water. As it disappeared Horace told me, "He'll stay down for ten minutes or so. No use looking for him in any particular direction because they

move like lightning under the water, and you never know where they'll come up next." My reaction was identical to Cabot's when he had been told the same thing so many years earlier. I thought to myself: "He'll probably come up right under this boat!"

But when the grampus surfaced again, it was far away from us; and we landed on the beach without mishap. We were on the seaward edge of a crescent of land about five miles long called Garland Bight. Horace, Robert and I started along the beach. Our plan was to walk about a mile and a half to a trail that would take us three miles over a hill to Horace's camp on Frank's Brook, a stream that runs into the bay. From there we would take Horace's canoe up the brook to an unnamed waterfall that had presented the first obstacle to the earlier explorers.

Our little expedition would afford us a close look at a rich variety of natural phenomena—those of the beach, of the boreal woodland on the hill, of the river and its shore. Moreover, it would take us through a typically Labradorian landscape: a transition area between the boreal woodland along the coast and the barren tundra farther inland. Less spectacular in summer than it is during the winter (see Chapter 6), this transition belt includes flora and fauna of both areas.

As we walked along the beach, we could see a flight of black guillemots rise from a sandbar far out in the bay. These year-round inhabi-

WOLF TRACKS IN THE SAND

tants of the rocky coast are the size and shape of a pigeon, with the diving habits of a loon. We stopped to watch them, but they refused to fly within camera range. We had just moved on again when Horace stopped and said, "There's your wolf."

Sure enough, a little way up the beach was a string of fresh wolf tracks. It was "my" wolf because, as we approached in the boat, I had spotted a white animal scrambling up the hillside. It disappeared into the brush before I could call Horace's attention to it. He identified it as a wolf even without seeing it. When I asked him how he could be so sure, he explained that it had to be a wolf because it did not look back at us. The wolf, he claimed, is the only Labrador animal that never takes a backward glance.

THE BEACH AT VOISEY BAY

SEABEACH SANDWORT

MOUNTAIN CRANBERRY

The tracks were those of a fully-grown animal. Horace recalled that he had come across the tracks of one small and one large wolf near his cabin the day before. This led him to believe that a family of wolves, inhabitants alike of the forest and the tundra, had moved into the area. Evidently the animal that had left these tracks on the beach was not a lone wolf but a father or mother out hunting food for its young.

From a willow clump near the beach came a cacophony of bird calls; although we could not see them, we could make out the voices of redpolls, crossbills and chickadees. We turned inland from the beach and walked towards the hill. As we did, we spotted a patch of seabeach sandwort. True to its name, it was sprouting in the gravel between the edge of the sandy beach and the beginning of the soil farther inland.

The sandwort was far north of its normal environment, and was growing here because the forest extends in a narrow belt along the coastline, farther north than it does in Labrador's interior. Even the cold Labrador Current makes for a slightly more temperate climate along the shore than that of the harsh interior. Still, while it was high summer in

WHITE-CROWNED SPARROW

most of North America, here on the 57th Parallel it was like early spring, with patches of snow clinging to the hills, and the sandwort had just begun to bloom.

The wooded area at the foot of the hill was dotted with flowering shrubs typical of the countryside at the edge of the tundra: all were members of the rugged heath family. There were blueberries, bear-berries, mountain cranberries. And because of the brief growing season in Labrador, the mountain cranberry plants were simultaneously producing both flowers and fruit.

The mountain cranberry's bell-shaped flowers, of a nearly diaphanous white tinged with pink, were incredibly delicate. I marvelled that anything so fragile should survive in this chilling environment. But for all its apparent frailty, the mountain cranberry is a tough specimen. It belongs to the genus *Vaccinium*, fossilized specimens of which have been discovered in strata of rock predating the latest Ice Ages. Here, where it seemed as if the Ice Ages had just passed, these dainty little flowers were right at home.

We passed a grove of speckled alders, where some small birds were feeding on the innumerable seeds produced by these prolific shrubs. The birds were sparrows—but a species with a special affinity for the north: they were white-crowned sparrows which withstand Labrador's climate and shun tall trees, preferring alder and willow bushes and the dwarf bushes that grow near the beginning of the tundra.

A Hill 7,000 Years Old

With the tinkling calls of the sparrows behind us, we started up the hill. It was a moraine, composed of glacial sediment deposited by the Labradorian ice that covered the area 17,000 years ago and retreated 7,000 years ago. As it receded, a huge glacier must have broken to pieces in this area, squeezing the earth into elongated hills such as this one.

It was a hard climb; but Horace, although in his fifties, showed no sign of exertion; he has lived in this wilderness most of his life. Still, after we gained the crest of the hill, we paused for a minute to take in the panoramic view of the bay behind us. When we resumed our walk, Horace called over his shoulder: "I've got a surprise for you." He led the way to a clearing. Here, in the Labrador bush, was a stretch of desert, complete with sand dunes.

THE BAY FROM THE TOP OF THE MORAINE

This barren basin of sand, about 200 feet in diameter, provided an example of the effect the climate can have on the face of Labrador. Ice, snow and rain had devastated the topsoil in the area. As soon as funnel-like openings appeared in the bush, the relentless winds bored through them and uprooted the vegetation. With nothing left to bind it, the topsoil was blown away, exposing the sand underneath. Then the swirling winds gradually carved out a depression, laying bare all the area within it.

Because of the way they are formed by the winds, such mini-deserts are known to soil scientists as "blow-outs"; winds had also exposed the roots of the trees and had then knocked them down.

I walked over to look at the trees still standing at the periphery. The bark of some of them had been blasted off by the blowing sand, and the wood underneath had been polished smooth. They would not stand much longer; some of their roots had already been exposed. I could see where the wind-driven sand was beginning to encroach on them. Over the months and years the surrounding circle of trees would succumb and topple, the sand would drift over them and the desert area would expand. Only when the sand dunes rose high enough to shield the growth behind them, would the spread of devastation be halted.

Here was the one area where I had to revise my theory that I was witnessing the same landscape that Labrador's earlier explorers had come upon. Erosion of this sort can change a vista relatively quickly. The blow-out we were looking at may well have been a grove of trees only a few decades ago.

Along a Caribou Trail

Now we headed into the boreal woodland that extended inland to the edge of the tundra. That barren area started beyond the waterfall which was our destination. Our trail through this park-like country of black and white spruces and tamaracks followed the track of a recent caribou migration. It was covered with the mainstay of the animal's diet, the woven lichen that is known as caribou moss.

The spaciousness of the boreal woodland is caused to some extent by the casualty rate of the trees in such an area. The caribou moss piles up so thickly that it is difficult for the trees to take root in it; and shallow-rooted trees are likely to be blown over or knocked down by other falling trees. Along the caribou trail we came to a spot where it looked as if some baby white spruces had managed to put down roots. But on closer examination this proved to be another of Labrador's endless deceptions. The "trees" turned out to be a form of herb called club-moss, which looks amazingly like a set of tiny evergreens.

A "BLOW-OUT" IN THE BUSH

LABRADOR TEA BLOSSOMS

CLUB-MOSS GROWING IN CARIBOU MOSS

ness was actually the scene of a great deal of activity. Horace pointed out a fox burrow under a tree; our path was criss-crossed with well-worn, utterly straight squirrel tracks. In the middle of the trail we came upon a broken caribou antler. Obviously, a couple of bull caribou had once fought it out at this spot. About a mile farther on, near Horace's camp, we found a pile of faded, whitish fur. "A wolf must have dragged a caribou leg up here to eat it," Horace explained.

We reached his camp on Frank's Brook by about 1.00 p.m., and had a typical Labrador lunch of fried Arctic char, with preserved partridge

Unlike the trees, the low-lying heath shrubs have no difficulty existing in the boreal woodland. They seem to be able to grow in almost solid rock. The most common of these wide-spread heath shrubs is appropriately named Labrador Tea. It has tiny white clustered blossoms and emits a pleasant fragrance. In spite of its name, incidentally, Labrador Tea does not make very good tea, although the Indians sometimes boil the leaves to be used as medicine.

By the time we were in mid-forest the sun was high and it was getting hot. We took some resin from the black spruces and chewed it like gum, to keep our mouths moist. Although we encountered little wildlife on the rest of the trail, except for the ubiquitous, noisy Canada jays, we did encounter ample evidence that this seemingly tranquil wilder-

THE MOSS-CARPETED FOREST TRAIL

TAMARACKS ON THE RIVER BANK

chewed off, probably by a squirrel.

Labrador is the last place I would expect to find a delicate flower resembling an orchid. Yet here, flowering in the cold shade of a river bank were what looked almost like hot-house orchids. Actually they were mountain heath, members of the same hardy heath family as the Labrador Tea; the heaths grow as far north as any plant on earth. Heaths are the predominant flower of Labrador, and indeed are the chief vegetation of the colder wastelands in other parts of the world. But Labrador is one of the coldest, and of the 3,500 members of the heath family, only 31 are sturdy enough to grow here. A worse enemy of the heath family is heat;

berries for a sweet. Then, rested and refreshed, we took the canoe and headed upriver. Only in a place as big as Labrador, I reflected, would a waterway 250 feet wide be called a brook.

Along the banks we could see the impact of erosion of a different kind from that which we had witnessed in the little desert caused by the blow-out. Here the erosion was the scouring action of rushing water, combined with the pressure of ice in winter and the buffeting of the broken ice in the spring. This force had undermined the sandy river bank, causing more and more of it to slide into the water each year.

The trees growing along the bank had gone down with the soil. Many had lost their footholds and fallen into the water. But some were im-

pressively resilient. Although they had slid and toppled so that their trunks were nearly parallel to the water and only a few feet above it, they had resumed growing upwards towards the sun, like the arm of a man flexing his muscles.

A Hardy Heath

About a mile and a half up the river we drew our canoe on to a natural landing and went for a walk in the woods along the shore. Here the swamp laurel was flowering in gorgeous profusion. In the farming country of southern Canada a dead ringer for this heath shrub is known as lambkill, because the leaves contain a toxin that poisons sheep. But the Labrador swamp laurel is a different species, and Labrador animals eat it without any ill effect. I saw a plant with its leaves partly

SWAMP LAUREL

practically no heaths exist in the continental United States for example, and most of these grow on mountain tops.

Another example of Labrador's many deceptions is the false strawberry, which we found flowering amid the caribou moss and British soldier lichens. The false strawberry is actually a three-toothed cinquefoil; the strawberry appellation refers to the shape of its leaves, which resemble those of the true strawberry. In addition, whereas the flowers of most cinquefoils are yellow, these are white. Thus they can easily be confused with the flowers of the wild strawberry. Furthermore, cinquefoils are members of the rose family, to which the strawberry also belongs; so the false and true strawberries are, in fact, close relations to each other.

We returned for another spell on the river, and Horace pulled over to a rocky point on a stretch of fast water. He pointed to a pool where the water slowed down somewhat. "Trout," he said. By this time it was mid-afternoon, the sun was bright, and it took a while for my eyes to adjust and see beneath the surface of the shimmering water. Then I could make out a plump speckled trout basking in the pool. From time to time one trout would dart off and another, or two or three, would take its place. I guessed that some of these fish must have weighed three pounds or more and measured two feet long—an impressive size for a trout. At length a layer of foam began to build up on the surface of

MOUNTAIN HEATH

FALSE STRAWBERRY

the water, and these splendid creatures were lost to my sight.

The foam floating down the surface of the river was the first indication that we were approaching a waterfall. Now I became aware of the rumbling thunder up ahead of us. We were still three-quarters of a mile from the waterfall, with many bends in the river to round before we would see it. The sound of the plunging water was muffled by the remaining trees along the riverbank. But already we could see that the trees were thinning out; and the roar of the falls increased as we proceeded upriver.

We paddled past a sandbank overgrown with golden willow bushes, where a speckled sandpiper skittered along the beach. In the middle of the stream was another example of the timeless process of erosion. An island of jagged boul-

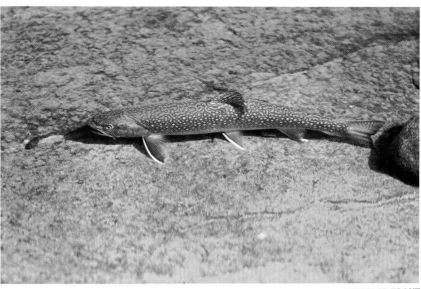

SPECKLED TROUT

ders sat amid a stretch of rapids. Once they had been solid rock. But over thousands of years the unremitting assault of ice, waterborne rock and the river's flow had broken the one large rock into the many smaller rocks through which the stream now flowed, carrying us along with a rush.

Below the rapids we stopped again to look at more fish. The Arctic char had begun to come up the river on their annual migration. The char is midway in size between a speckled trout and an Atlantic salmon. These char flashed past us so swiftly that we were able to catch only momentary glimpses of them.

The rumble of the falls was much louder now. But before approaching the cataract in the canoe, Horace wanted us to see the portage that the explorers used a century ago and trappers still use to get around this awesome obstacle. We climbed a long path at about a 45° angle; I was glad we were not carrying the canoe.

Along the way we could hear a woodpecker trip-hammering a hole into a dead tree. At the top of the trail was an area that had been burned over by a forest fire. Horace pointed out where the wind off the river had blown the fire back on itself and halted its spread.

What was spared from the fire was thinning vegetation. We had reached the edge of the boreal woodland, consisting only of low-lying shrubs and the hardiest trees —mostly spruce, with a few tamaracks. The lichens and mosses were taking over; on the tundra they and a few grasses and sedges would be the only growing things.

The mosquitoes had been out in vast numbers during the land-bound portions of our trip, and when we reached the hilltop they were appalling. Every time Robert stopped to take a picture, so many mosquitoes landed on his light tan jacket that it turned dark grey. We decided not to linger and back-tracked to the canoe.

There were more flecks of foam on the water as we pulled out into the mainstream. The river became choppier as we moved along towards the falls and it became harder to control the canoe. We still could not see the waterfall, up ahead of us, but I could tell from the increasing thunder, the foam and the churning surface of the river that we were getting close. By now the water had millions of little bubbles in it, as if it had come to the boil.

A Thundering Cascade

We rounded a bend and there it was. Thousands of tons of water were rolling and roaring and cascading over a 100-foot drop from the river above to where we were paddling below. Moving into the ambit of the waterfall was like being caught in a rainstorm. Its mists created its own rain, and its own ceaseless thunder. As the water tumbled around us on its way from the great Labrador plateau to the ocean, I felt very small and vulnerable. I was relieved when Horace finally swung the canoe away from the waterfall's roaring maw, and the rushing current began to carry us easily back downstream.

WAVES AND MIST AT THE WATERFALL

4/ The Little Creatures

There is a kind of small fly or gnat that stingeth and offendeth sorely, leaving many red spots on the face and other places where she stingeth.

RICHARD HAKLUYT/ *DIVERS VOYAGES TOUCHING THE DISCOVERY OF AMERICA*

Labrador is such a big and open place that you almost expect all its fauna to be outsized. Of course, it has its share of big animals, but it is also the domain of thousands of species of little creatures—from furtive voles and lemmings to aggressive flies and mosquitoes.

Most of the tiny fauna cannot readily be seen, especially in winter. The scenery certainly seemed empty to me one winter evening when I was snowshoeing down a broad, white river valley a few miles above Churchill Falls in search of nocturnal fauna. The night was clear and soundless, and the temperature was well below zero. The only noise was the *scrinch, scrunch, scrinch, scrunch* of my snowshoes padding mile after mile over the snow. A brilliant ceiling of stars provided a jewelled accompaniment to a spectacular display of Northern Lights. Briefly I felt the supreme and special sense of solitude that is possible only in the most remote areas of the world. But I knew I was not really alone; there was life underneath this silent snow.

Under my big bear-paw snowshoes the snow sounded hollow, as if I were walking over a roof. In a way I was, for a snowfield is not always the monolithic mass it appears to be. A few inches below the compost crust the snow crystals are more loosely packed. If you dig through this stuff, you find that, as you go deeper, the crystals are farther apart from each other. At the very bottom, especially around the trunks of trees and roots of bushes, there are small caverns of air space between the snow and the ground. In certain spots you can discover small tunnels branching out from these caverns, both along the ground and upwards through the snow pack to the surface. These burrows are the relatively safe and comfortable homes of some of the best-hidden little creatures of the northern winter: the collared lemmings and red-backed voles, two closely-related, mouse-like species.

The temperature under the insulating blanket of snow is often as much as 40°F. higher than it is on the surface. No matter how cold it gets above the snow cover, the temperature next to the ground stays around 18°F. That's because some heat always rises from the molten interior of the earth. The slow application of this warmth causes the snow closest to the ground to evaporate.

In the air spaces thus created the under-snow animals can breathe. They are especially equipped by nature for this environment: they emit little carbon dioxide and thus, unlike other mammals, are not subject to asphyxiation from lack of sufficient oxygen. To find sustenance, the lemmings and voles burrow through the snow, making tunnels along the ground from one cavern to another. In the caverns they gather stores of dead grass and leaves, dried-up berries, seeds and lichens. They supplement this litter with what nourishment they can obtain by gnawing at the bark of shrubs.

The voles' and lemmings' active winter life underground is an adaptation unlike that of most other little creatures of Labrador. Squirrels, woodchucks and most types of mice spend the winter months confined to their lairs, living off their own fat or food they have stored away. But while the lemmings and voles continue to forage in their snow tunnels, their hidden existence does not itself protect them from all predators. The weasel searches out the entrances and exits to their burrows, slinks through them, and pounces on the trapped prey. The larger martens and foxes locate them by listening for their movements below the snow and dig down into the snow tunnels.

These wild rodents would be a lot safer were it not for their urge to take an occasional excursion to the surface. If you look carefully around a snowfield, you may see their neat little exit holes, usually alongside a tree or shrub. The rodents use them to surface for a look around or to skitter about gathering seeds and other debris that have fallen on top of the snow. Such excursions can lead to a quick end in the clutches of a mink or a marten or one of the numerous species of owls that hungrily patrol the forest and tundra in winter. The vole has a habit of coming out in the evening and at night when the great horned owl is at its most alert. The collared lemming may pop up at any time of day; and when it surfaces in daylight, it is easy prey for the snowy owl. Unlike most of its kind, the snowy owl—whose habitat is the northern tundra—hunts around the clock.

The Labrador lemming (*Dicrostonyx hudsonius*) also provides periodic feasts for the snowy owl and other predators in a curious and well publicized way. Like other lemmings, it has a cyclical instinct to swarm across the countryside. The phenomenon is thought to occur every three or four years, and to be caused by the pressures of overpopulation. The crowding of their territories makes the lemmings panic and run aimlessly about in vast numbers. During these mysterious stampedes, the lemmings' predators gorge themselves. The following year the surviving lemmings begin their population growth all over again, and meanwhile their predators are forced to expand their range south, where there is a greater variety of prey.

But on this still night as I snowshoed along the forest trail nothing seemed to be stirring. Evidently even the owls were resting. The ptarmigan and grouse were in their sleeping burrows. (They make them by flying headlong into the snow.) Some chickadees remain in Labrador all winter, but if there were any about, they were huddled in their holes in the trees. Snowshoe hares are usually active at night, as are their prime natural enemies, the Canada lynxes; but it looked to me as if even the hares were asleep.

I had begun my journey late in the afternoon, and it was now about 9 p.m.; it had been dark for nearly five hours. What a fantastic contrast with summer, I thought. At this hour in July it would still be broad daylight. This same silent trail would be noisy with the chirping of returned migratory redstarts, fox sparrows, juncos and several varieties of thrushes. The frogs would be starting their nightly sing-song in the marshes. The trout would be jumping in the lake. And far from needing to seek out the natural life in Labrador, I would be constantly encountering more of it than I would want.

Among the hardiest and most prevalent of Labrador's little creatures is a hump-backed villain that is prosaically known as the black fly. This insect spends the winter as a tiny, greenish-brown egg attached by a disc-like sucker to a rock, reed or deadfall in a river or stream. With spring's lengthening days, the egg changes to a larva, which absorbs nutriments and oxygen through its body surface, growing to the pupal stage in three weeks. In much of Labrador this period usually

A snowy owl, well camouflaged for its predatory role, watches from a winter branch for a tender vole or lemming to emerge from a passageway beneath the snow. Unlike most other owls, this particular species hunts by day as well as night.

runs from the last week in May to mid-June. That short span of only three weeks—between the end of winter and the beginning of the fly season—is the best time to visit Labrador.

The first insect assault of each year is launched by a tiny type of black fly nicknamed "No-see-'em". The sobriquet is a bit inaccurate, because you can see 'em all right—they sometimes travel in hordes so dense that in the distance they look like the smoke from a forest fire. Closer-up, however, because of their infinitesimal size and light brown colour, they are indeed almost invisible individually. You don't feel 'em much, either, when they bite—but you do later. I recall walking along a riverbank in late June, near Happy Valley in the more southerly part of Labrador, where it still looked and felt like April in southern Canada. There was hard snow in the crevices of rock, and the pussy willows and Labrador Tea bushes were just beginning to bud. Surely there could be no flies yet, I thought; and sure enough, I didn't see any. I had not taken the precaution of tucking my trousers into my boots as a defence against the flies, because it didn't seem necessary. Yet when I took off my boots that evening, I found an unbroken ring of itchy No-see-'em bites where the top of my socks ended. I hadn't seen any around my face or hands; "No-see-'ems" are insidious creatures.

The little black flies provide only a prelude for their bigger cousins. By July the bush country whines like a power saw with black flies that are about a quarter of an inch long. These tough-skinned insects breed two or three times during the summer and flourish in incredible profusion. Researchers who once tried to count the number of eggs on a 15-foot stretch of rock, beside a waterfall in northern Quebec near the Labrador border, estimated the number at 16 billion. More than 325 black flies a minute have been counted landing on a scrap of blue cloth less than a foot square. (Blue is their favourite colour; no one knows why.)

Black flies formidably influence human life in the wilder parts of the Canadian Shield country and deserve much of the credit for preserving Labrador as a wilderness. Because of the black flies, a Canadian woodsman in his summer clothes looks almost as if he were dressed for winter. He usually has a long-sleeved undershirt sticking out from the tightly buttoned cuffs of his shirt, which is also buttoned at the neck. If he is a real old-timer, he wears a suit of long underwear, even on the warmest days. His unspoken logic is that it is better to be a little overheated than to leave any openings for black flies. For the same reason, Labradorians wear hats and caps, and tuck their trousers into their boots. The trousers are usually green or tan-coloured. Blue jeans may be all right for cowboys and trendy teenagers, but not for anyone in the Labrador bush because of the black flies' preference for this colour. They also like all dark clothing, so experienced woodsmen stick to the lighter shades.

But there is no complete defence against these insects. They have a fantastic ability to get at any exposed part of the anatomy. I remember one particularly bad day, at the height of the fly season, when I was temporarily blinded by black flies covering both sides of my glasses. They crawled into my ears, up my nostrils, down my throat. My companion and I couldn't talk at lunch because every time we opened our mouths three or four flies would rush in; anyway, it was difficult to hear each other amid their steady buzzing. That was a memorable day for black flies, but only a little more so than usual for the Labrador bush.

It is difficult to believe, but only half—the female half—of the black-fly population bites, in order to obtain blood to nourish their eggs. The female's saw-edged mandibles work like a pair of pinking shears, tearing away a little piece of flesh with each bite. These gouges can bleed profusely. I once met a logger on a forest trail whose face looked like a raw beefsteak as the result of fly bites.

The fly's bite also leaves a touch of saliva in the wound. Although Labrador's black flies do not carry parasites or diseases, their saliva is toxic. On most people and animals it creates a small, itchy swelling that can easily become infected. Some people (and presumably some animals) have a more severe reaction to the toxin than others. Large doses can cause an illness called black-fly fever; the condition is characterized by headache, fever, nausea and swollen lymph glands. I have seen black-fly fever victims, and they looked very sick indeed. In extreme cases they develop large carbuncles where the bites have become infected, and go into a state of delirium. The Labrador cure for this is a poultice made from the bark of a tamarack tree which draws the pus from the carbuncle and reduces the fever.

Labradorians who have been exposed for generations seem to become relatively used to the black flies' attack. I have seen naked Indian children covered from head to toe with hundreds of bloody bites. Some say that this early exposure provides a certain amount of immunity in later life. I once stood on the shore of a lake with an Indian canoe-maker who reckoned he was 104 years old. Black flies were biting him as fiercely as they were me, but seemed to bother him a lot less.

Perhaps you can eventually get used to anything, even black flies, but it is an unnerving process. Grown men have been reduced to tears by the flies' persistent swarming, their sharp little bites and their sound.

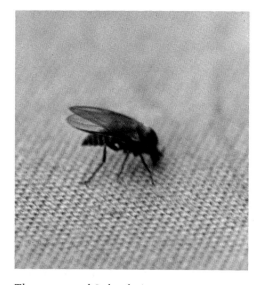

The scourge of Labrador's summer— but protector of the countryside as a wilderness—is the black fly (above), which infests Labrador throughout the short warm season, and makes the region inhospitable to all but the most resolute of inhabitants.

That inescapable, endless, loud, undulating buzzing can shred a man's nerves. Once, while a group of us were on a canoe trip, the flies were swarming around us as we tried to eat supper. One of the men suddenly flung his plate to the ground, ran down to the beach and plunged into the water, clothes and all. Thus relieved, he was soon laughing with us and at himself as he splashed around in the water. But sometimes it is no laughing matter. People have literally been driven out of their minds by the black flies' relentless attack.

Repellents that work on most insects do not seem to have much effect on Labrador's black flies. Labradorians are inclined to look askance at what they call "fly dope". One guide I travelled with told me that the best place for insect repellent is on a stump. "You smear it on the stump, see, and all the flies go to eat the stuff on the stump and leave you alone." I have found that one special liquid repellent with a very heavy concentration (more than 70 per cent) of a chemical called diethyltoluamide is effective if I keep reapplying it every few minutes. Most widely-used commercial brands of repellent have about 33 per cent of this chemical. But my super-strength fly dope tarnishes metal, turns certain types of plastic to gooey mush, and eats through synthetic fabrics. Presumably it does not do my skin much good.

In any case, perspiration soon dilutes the repellent or washes it away, and black flies will pounce on any unprotected piece of flesh, even a space as small as one exposed by a stream of perspiration. The best remedy I know of is the old Indian one of building a densely smoky smudge; but you can't spend all day crouching in a cloud of smoke. So Labradorians have no choice but to endure the black fly stoically as one of the vicissitudes of life.

For animals the fly plague can be even more serious. Dogs in Labrador regularly die of fly bites. Animals subject to a massive attack go into a state of shock; their muscles tremble uncontrollably and their breathing becomes heavy and jerky. They may die within 15 minutes to two hours. Black-fly attacks can also bring on severe disorientation in animals. Nursing females lose their milk; breeding is interrupted because of irritations to the genitals. No animal, big or small, is exempt. I have seen a bull moose go crashing through the bush towards water trying to escape them, and a black bear rolling over and over on a sandy road in an attempt to shake them off. There is evidence that black flies prey on turtles' noses, and even bite ants.

Although all black flies appear to bite everything that moves, some species are highly specialized feeders. One kind bites only ducks, and in fact can kill them; another confines itself exclusively to loons. I don't know whether or not there are black flies that bite other black flies, but it wouldn't surprise me if there were.

The black-fly season lasts longer in Labrador than in the rest of northern Canada. When I first asked a Labradorian the length of the black-fly season here, I got the laconic reply: "Break-up to first frost." In more temperate Canadian Shield areas the height of the season is usually past by mid-July. In Labrador (except in the far northern areas where the summer is shorter) the flies thrive without let-up from June to October. Moreover, while in most of northern Canada the black flies are at their worst during early morning and dusk, in Labrador they go after you throughout the daylight hours.

There may be more scientific reasons for the persistence of the Labrador black fly, but one obvious explanation is that Labrador contains more unbroken woodland than most parts of Canada, and black flies are always more numerous and active in forested than in open country. Another reason is their need for running water to incubate. More than one-third of Labrador is composed of water; it is awash in rivers, streams and brooks. And the water is cold throughout the summer, thus providing ideal conditions for the black flies to produce three or even four batches a year.

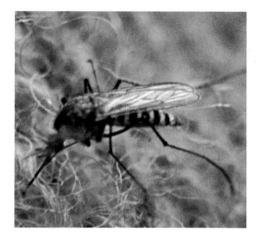

The voracious Labrador mosquito is a menace second only to the black fly. This one (above) is attempting to bore its way through a thick woollen sweater. The mosquitoes on the right swarm over a tent screen.

Yet Labrador's black flies are nearly matched by its mosquitoes. They, too, have helped protect Labrador from human incursion.

An observer of the Labrador mosquito was the British explorer H. Hesketh Prichard, who visited Labrador's bush in 1910. A Fellow of the Royal Geographical Society, Prichard in 1910 crossed northern Labrador from Nain to Indian House Lake, and then returned the same way. Here is one of his diary entries:

"August 13. . . . Went again for a walk to look for a stag. Saw mosquitoes. What these mosquitoes are is indescribable. They give no rest, no peace, day and night they go on and on and on. I think a man totally unprotected would be killed by them in a very short space of time. I remember reading somewhere that the Indians in the old days used to kill their Eskimo prisoners by exposing them naked to swarms of mosquitoes. It would be difficult to imagine anything more fiendish. . . . When one's clothes are drawn tight, they pierce through even two thicknesses of cloth and all along the seams. One is a mass of bites, tortured by lack of sleep, wracked with nerves."

Prichard was quite right in thinking that the mosquitoes could bite an

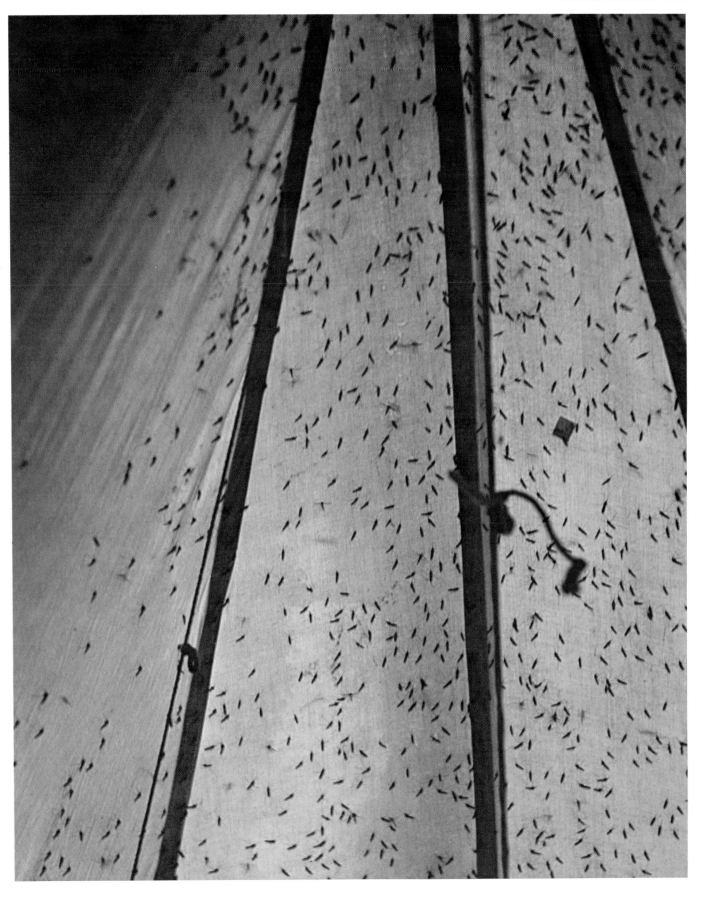

Only less numerous than the flies and mosquitoes, the well-named "Labrador bulldog", a northern version of the horse fly, delivers a memorable bite. One explorer claimed that the insects bit off chunks of his flesh and flew into the trees to chew on them.

unprotected man to death. Studies have shown that northern Canadian mosquitoes will attack a man's exposed forearm at a rate of 289 bites a minute. "Thus," wrote Professor J. G. Gillett, a British authority on the insect, extrapolating from the figure, "a totally unprotected man could receive more than 9,000 bites per minute, which would result in the loss of half his blood in less than two hours." His conclusion took into account the fact that a mosquito drinks in only two to eight milligrams of blood per "bite"—which is not an actual bite like that of the black fly, but a sucking process through a proboscis.

Although Labrador mosquitoes do not carry any known disease, they are capable of killing animals. They can penetrate through a moose's thin fur. If an animal's fur is too thick, they attack its eyes, rectum and genitals. The Indians tell of lynxes plunging to their deaths in the rapids of a river, apparently driven to desperation by mosquito attacks.

The mosquitoes of Labrador are most in their element on the barren tundra. There they whine around the caribou in such numbers that they cause the big animals to stampede. The resourceful Arctic fox has developed the technique of burying its face in the dust to avoid mosquito bites. Mammals, however, are generally scarce on the tundra, so the insects turn their attention to the many species of birds which breed in the far north. They can bite birds on the wing, in spite of evasive action. They are particularly successful against birds sitting on nests. An eider duck incubating eggs is literally a sitting duck for mosquito attacks around the eyes, which can blind it. At times, when the mosquitoes succeed in driving a duck away from its nest, they vainly assail the eggs.

As with the black fly, only the female mosquito attacks, piercing the skin like a hypodermic needle to obtain the "blood meal" she needs to nourish her eggs. "If only the female bites," Mrs. Ian Strachan, of Nain, once commented to me, "I don't think I've ever seen a male."

Since summer comes so late in Labrador, the chances are slim that the mosquito will get a blood meal to develop her first batch of eggs in the spring; but nature looks after that. Unlike most of the 2,400 species of mosquitoes around the world, the two most common types in Labrador do not necessarily need an infusion of blood in order for their first eggs to hatch. Northern mosquitoes spawn in stagnant water; their eggs are hardy enough to survive the winter beneath the ice, emerging as soon as the ice melts. There is even one species in Labrador that moves into the pupal and adult stages while still locked in the ice, so that it is all set to go with the first blush of spring.

I find some consolation in the fact that I can't recall ever seeing any great numbers of black flies and mosquitoes together. I gather that where there are numerous black flies, the mosquitoes restrict their activities mainly to the twilight hours and to night time, to the insides of tents and buildings and to the swampy parts of the bush. Perhaps these two insects tend to avoid each other. Labrador lore has it that both of them keep away from an even more formidable insect aptly called the "Labrador bulldog". This flying menace, akin to and the size of the southern horsefly, can take chunks out of your flesh with a bite nearly as painful as the sting of a bee. Several varieties of big flies are found in Labrador, and all of them are lumped together under the heading of "bulldogs". The most common seems to be *chrysops*, known in the rest of Canada as the deerfly. These insects abound throughout the warm weather months, especially near Labrador's streams and marshes. The fact that they normally prey on tough-skinned animals accounts for the viciousness of their bite. They are equipped with powerful mouthparts designed to penetrate a heavy coat of fur.

There is evidently a scarcity of insect predators in Labrador. I have noticed that there are few of the spiders that usually feed on mosquitoes and black flies. Only one species of insect-eating bat—the little brown bat—lives in Labrador's cold climate, and it is confined to the more southerly areas. There certainly are plenty of fly-eating birds in Labrador in the summer; but evidently not enough of them to put a dent in the population of the insects.

Still, there is an ample supply of one flying creature that I regard as man's best friend, because it does feed on black flies and mosquitoes; I hate to think how many flies and mosquitoes there would be in Labrador without the dragonfly. It is sometimes called "the fisherman's companion"; I suspect that the dragonfly hangs around fishermen because men attract flies.

I recently spent a couple of evening hours on the shore of a lake near Churchill Falls, watching dragonflies at work. The trout were making the water boil as they broke the surface to catch insects. But the dragonflies were more efficient. The dragonfly is a well equipped insect-killer. Hovering tirelessly like a helicopter on its double sets of wings, it uses its long front legs like a basket to scoop up flies and mosquitoes and devours them without a tremor while still in flight. The dragonfly has a direct digestive system consisting of a canal from the mouth to the anus, and readily consumes a phenomenal number of black flies and mosquitoes; dragonflies have been found with more than a hundred mosquitoes in their mouths at one time.

In fact, the dragonfly performs its useful function in two phases of its life cycle. That evening I had the chance to observe both phases. Out on the lake the adult dragonflies were making passes over the same point again and again; evidently a hatch of flies or mosquitoes was rising there. Meanwhile, in a small stagnant puddle at the edge of a little brook that emptied into the lake, dragonfly nymphs were at work.

These immature dragonflies are dun-coloured, wingless bugs. In the little pond they were crawling along the bottom, feeding on mosquito and fly eggs; they can consume at least a score a minute. The nymph uses a form of jet propulsion; it draws water into its tail through a breathing vent and expels it to shoot forward through the water. At the same time it unfolds a lower "lip", about one-third the length of its body, from its normal resting position over its face; with this lip it reaches out for its prey. At the end of this hinged device is a set of pincers that grab the victim and hold it tight. The big lip then folds back and stuffs the prey into the nymph's mouth. It would make a chilling scene for a horror movie if it could be sufficiently magnified.

What I was watching was one stage in the immensely complex food relationships that govern life in the wilds. A short and simple food chain of this sort would begin with microscopic algae, which are consumed by slightly larger protozoans, which are consumed by black-fly larvae and water beetles, both of which are consumed by dragonfly nymphs. Related food chains could branch out in any number of directions from here, but let me try to keep it simple and straightforward.

In the shallows where the brook emptied into the lake, I saw a shoal of little fish. These were probably baby speckled trout, which would soon be big enough to eat dragonfly nymphs. When the trout grow up, they will share a community of interest with the dragonflies that have emerged from the nymphs. Both the mature trout and the dragonflies feed on mosquitoes, black flies and other insect life along the lakeshore. The trout play their part in the food chain, both feeding on insects and providing food for those next in the chain: ospreys cruise over the water, watching for the flashing bodies of fish swimming up to the surface. The bird selects one fish, times its dive to coincide with the rising of the fish, and comes up with a fat trout in its claws.

So there you have a short and simple food chain: algae-to-protozoan-to-water beetle-to dragonfly nymph-to-trout-to-osprey. A similar food chain on land includes the seeds and berries that are eaten by the voles, lemmings and other rodents, which are eaten in turn by weasels and martens. The little, wild rodents are the lynchpins of an elaborate system that extends from sunlight, which is the essential element in producing the vegetation they eat, to the wolf and the other big and powerful creatures of the wilds.

But nature in Labrador is not without its irony, for in the end the little creatures can dominate the system. Tiny parasites will kill a wolf, a wolverine or a caribou. A deadly germ that spreads among the snowshoe hares can ultimately decimate the population of the lynx which live mainly on hares. And consider this scenario: dragonfly eats black fly, trout eats dragonfly, otter eats trout, fox eats otter, lynx kills fox, man kills lynx. But black fly feeds on otter, fox, lynx and man—and prevents the latter, in the absence of very strong inducements, from invading its territory in sufficient numbers to threaten the rest of the wildlife population. Who, then, is the lord of the wilderness after all?

5/ An Eloquent Observer

*From the top of a high rock I had a fine view of the most
extensive and dreariest wilderness I have ever beheld.
It chilled the heart to gaze on these barren lands of Labrador.*

JOHN JAMES AUDUBON/ *LABRADOR JOURNAL*

In the flowing romantic dress of the
early 19th Century, John James
Audubon was portrayed eight years
after the Labrador expedition by his
son John. A member of the expedition,
young John added some bird portraits
of his own to those made by his father.

*Of all the early explorers of the Labrador Peninsula, none left a more
vivid record of his experience than the famous observer of birds, John
James Audubon. In the spring of 1833, Audubon chartered the schooner
Ripley in Eastport, Maine. Accompanied by five young naturalists, one
of them his son John, he set sail from Eastport on June 6 to sketch and
study the birds of the Labrador region. By June 14, Ripley was
approaching the southern coast of the Labrador Peninsula. For the next
month Audubon and his assistants cruised through this area (since
1927 it has been part of Quebec Province, but it was then known as
Labrador). Some bird species they captured; some they shot: it was still
the tradition, as in Darwin's time, to seize or kill a specimen in order to
examine it exhaustively.*

*Audubon also kept an informal journal, in which he eloquently
described Labrador's austere beauty and ferocious weather. Here and
on the following pages are excerpts from that journal, starting with
Ripley's arrival at Gannet Rock, a famous bird island off the peninsula's
southern coast. A selection of the striking bird portraits that resulted
from the expedition is presented on pages 136-149.*

June 14, off Gannet Rock. Our pilot, a Mr. Godwin from Nova Scotia,
put the vessel towards an island where he told us that Gannets bred in
great numbers. For several days past we have met with an increased
number of Gannets, and as we sailed this morning we observed long and
numerous files. Their flight now was low above the water, forming easy
undulations, flapping thirty or forty times, and then gliding about the

same distance; these were all returning from fishing, and were gorged with food for their mates or young.

About ten a speck rose on the horizon, the breeze increased fast, and we neared this object apace. At eleven I could distinguish its top plainly from the deck, and thought it covered with snow to the depth of several feet. What we saw was not snow—but Gannets! I rubbed my eyes, took my spy-glass, and in an instant the strangest picture stood before me. They were birds we saw—a mass of birds of such a size as I never before cast my eyes on. The whole of my party stood astounded and amazed.

The nearer we approached, the greater our surprise at the enormous number of these birds, all calmly seated on their eggs or newly hatched brood, their heads all turned to windward, and towards us. The air above for a hundred yards, and for some distance around the whole rock, was filled with Gannets on the wing.

The birds, which we could now see distinctly, sat almost touching each other and in regular lines. Godwin tells me the top of the rock is about a quarter of a mile wide, north and south, and a little narrower east to west; its elevation above the sea between three and four hundred feet. The sea beats round it with great violence, except after long calms, and it is extremely difficult to land upon it.

The whole surface is perfectly covered with nests, placed about two feet apart, in such regular order that you may look through the lines as you would look through a planted patch of sweet potatoes or cabbages.

The eggs are pure white, and as large as those of a Goose. By the 20th of May the rock is already covered with birds and eggs; about the 20th of June they begin to hatch. When the young are hatched they are black, and for a fortnight or more the skin looks like that of the dog-fish. Gradually they become downy and white, and when two months old look much like young lambs.

A great number of Kittiwake Gulls breed on this rock, with thousands of Foolish Guillemots. The Kittiwake makes its nest of eel-weeds, several inches in thickness, and in places too small for a Gannet or a Guillemot to place itself; in some instances these nests projected some inches over the edge of the rock. We could not see any of their eggs.

The stench from the rock is insufferable, as it is covered with the remains of putrid fish, rotten eggs, and dead birds, old and young. No man who has not seen what we have this day can form the least idea of the impression the sight made on our minds. By dark it blew a gale and we are now most of us rather shaky.

June 15. All our party except Coolidge were deadly sick. The thermometer was down to 43°F, and every sailor complained of the cold.

It has rained almost all day, I felt so very sick this morning that I removed from my berth to a hammock, where I soon felt rather more easy. We lay to all this time, and at daylight were in sight of the Island of Anticosti, distant about twenty miles; but fog came soon after and became so thick that nothing could be observed.

June 16, Sunday. The weather clear, beautiful, and much warmer; but it was calm, so we fished for cod, of which we caught a good many; most of them contained crabs of a curious sort, and some were filled with shrimps. One cod measured three feet six-and-a-half inches, and weighed twenty-one pounds.

June 17. I was on deck at three this morning. The sea was literally covered with Foolish Guillemots, playing in the very spray of the bow of our vessel, plunging under it, as if in fun.

I looked on our landing on the coast of Labrador as a matter of great importance. My thoughts were filled, not with airy castles, but with expectations of the new knowledge of birds and quadrupeds which I hoped to acquire. Our vessel, the *Ripley*, ploughed the deep, and proceeded swiftly on her way; she always sails well.

The air was filled with Velvet Ducks; *millions* of these birds were flying from the north-west towards the south-east. The Foolish Guillemots and the Razor-billed Auk were in immense numbers, flying in long files a few yards above the water with rather undulating motions, and passing within good gunshot of the vessel, now and then rounding to us, as if about to land on the very deck.

We went on to American Harbor, and after a while came to anchor in a small bay, perfectly secure from any winds. And now we are positively on the Labrador coast, latitude 50° and a little more: farther north than I ever was before. But what a country!

When we landed and passed the beach, we sank nearly up to our knees in mosses of various sorts, producing as we moved through them a curious sensation. These mosses, which at a distance look like hard rocks, are, under foot, like a velvet cushion.

We visited all the islands about the harbor; they were all rocky, nothing but rocks. The Great Black-backed Gull was sailing magnificently all about us. The Great Tern was plunging after shrimps in every pool, and we found four eggs of the Spotted Sandpiper. The nest was situated under a rock in the grass, and made of a quantity of dried grass, forming a very decided nest, at least much more so than in the middle United States, where the species breed so abundantly.

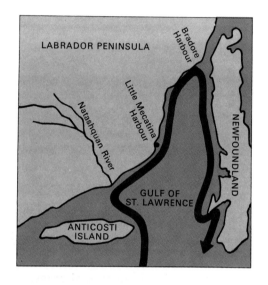

Ripley's route took the Audubon expedition up into the Gulf of St. Lawrence and as far north as Bradore (which Audubon spelled "Bras d'or") along the southern coast of the Labrador Peninsula. Now officially a part of Quebec, this area was then regarded as part of Labrador. On the return leg the party put into ports along the Labrador coast and that of Newfoundland which were then unknown to Audubon or still unnamed.

June 18. Our boats went off to some islands eight or ten miles distant, after birds and eggs, but the day, although very beautiful, did not prove valuable to us, as some eggers from Halifax had robbed these places.

Many nests of the Eider Duck were seen, some at the edge of the woods, placed under the rampant boughs of the fir trees, which in this latitude grow only a few inches above the surface of the ground; to find the nest, these boughs had to be raised. The nests were scooped a few inches deep in the mossy, rotten substance that forms here what must be called earth; the eggs are deposited on a bed of down and covered with the same material; and so warm are these nests that, although not a parent bird was seen near them, the eggs were quite warm to the touch, and the chicks in some actually hatching in the absence of the mother. Some of the nests had the eggs uncovered; six eggs was the greatest number found in a nest. The nests on grassy islands are fashioned in the same manner, and generally placed at the foot of a large tussock of grass.

John found many nests of the Great Black-backed Gull. The nest of this fine bird is made of mosses and grasses, raised on the solid rock, and handsomely formed within; a few feathers are in this lining. In the nest there were three eggs, large, hard-shelled, dirty yellowish, splashed and spotted with dark umber and black.

June 19. Drawing as much as the disagreeable motion of the vessel would allow me to do; and although at anchor and in a good harbor, I could scarcely steady my pencil, the wind being high from south-west. At three A.M. I had all the young men up, and they left by four for some islands where the Great Black-backed Gull breeds. When John returned he brought eight Auks and four of their eggs; these eggs measure three inches in length, one and seven-eighths in breadth, dirty-white ground, broadly splashed with deep brown and black. This Auk feeds on small fish, flies swiftly with a quick beat of the wings, rounding to and fro at the distance of fifty or more yards, exhibiting, as it turns, the pure white of its lower parts, or the jet black of its upper.

Five young Great Black-backed Gulls were brought back alive, small and beautifully spotted over the head and back, somewhat like a Leopard; they walked well about the deck, and managed to pick up the food given them. Their cry was a "hac, hac, hac, wheet, wheet, wheet". Frequently, when one was about to swallow a piece of flesh, a brother or sister would jump at it, tug, and finally deprive its relative of the morsel in an instant.

June 21. I drew all day an adult Gannet which we had brought from the great rock of which I have spoken. Many eggs of the Arctic Tern were collected to-day, two or three in a nest. These birds are as shy here as all others, and the moment John and Coolidge landed, or indeed approached the islands on which they breed, they all rose in the air, passed high overhead, screaming and scolding all the time the young men were on the land.

When our captain returned he brought about a dozen female Eider Ducks, a great number of their eggs, and a bag of down. The female draws the down from her abdomen as far towards her breast as her bill will allow her to, but the *feathers* are not pulled, and on examination of several specimens I found these cleaned from their original down, as a forest of trees is cleared of its undergrowth. In this state the female is still well clothed, and little or no difference can be seen in the plumage unless closely examined.

These birds have now nearly all hatched in this latitude, but we are told that we shall over-reach them and meet with nests and eggs as we go northeast until August.

The Wild Goose is an excellent diver, and when with its young uses many beautiful stratagems to save its brood, and elude the hunter. They will dive and lead their young under the surface of the water, and always in a contrary direction to the one expected; thus if you row a boat after one it will dive under it, and now and then remain under several minutes, while the hunter with outstretched neck; is looking, all in vain, for the *stupid Goose!* Every time I read or hear of a stupid animal in a wild state, I cannot help wishing that the stupid animal who speaks thus, was half as wise as the brute he despises.

I found many small flowers open this day, where none appeared last evening. All vegetable life here is of the pygmy order, and so ephemeral that it blooms, fructifies, and dies in a few weeks.

June 22. It was very rainy, and thermometer 54°F. After breakfast I dressed in my oilskins and went with the captain in the whaleboat to the settlement at the entrance of the Natasquan [Natashquan] River, five miles east. On our way we saw numerous Seals; these rise to the surface, erect the head to the full length of the neck, sniff the air, and you also, and sink back to avoid any further acquaintance with man.

June 23. I have sketched all day, at the background of the picture of Gannets [see pages 148-149]. John and party went off about six miles, and returned with half-a-dozen Guillemots, and ten or twelve dozen eggs. Coolidge brought in Arctic Terns and Great Black-backed Gulls; two young of the latter about three weeks old, having the same voice

The eider duck's nest (above) fascinated Audubon because of its lining of down which the female (right) plucked from her abdomen. He also found that one-week-old eider ducklings already were "thickly covered with a soft and warm down".

While going ashore to investigate Labrador's bird life, Audubon and party were themselves investigated by seals like those above. Inquisitive creatures, the harp seals of Labrador frequently rise from the water, look about and noiselessly sink below the surface. The seals gather on Labrador's ice floes (left) in winter. They mate and give birth here, and in summer return north, some of them travelling as far as the Arctic Circle.

and notes as the old ones. When on board they ran about the deck, and fed themselves with pieces of fish thrown to them. These young Gulls sit with their feet extended before them in an awkward-looking position, but one which to them is no doubt comfortable.

June 25. Bank Swallows in sight this moment, with the weather thick, foggy, and an east wind; where are these delicate pilgrims bound? The Black-poll Warbler is more abundant, and forever singing, if the noise it makes can be called a song. The sound resembles the clicking of small pebbles together five or six times.

June 27. It rained quite hard when I awoke this morning; the fog was so thick that the very shores of our harbor, not distant more than a hundred yards, were enveloped in gloom.

June 29. [At an island.] We found the Common Puffin breeding in great numbers. On this island their burrows are dug in the light black loam formed of decayed moss, three to six feet deep, yet not more than about a foot under the surface. The burrows ran in all directions, and in some instances connected; the end of the burrow is rounded, and there is the pure white egg. Those caught at the holes bit us furiously and scratched shockingly with the inner claw, making a mournful noise all the time. The whole island was perforated with their burrows.

July 1. We have had three Puffins on board, these three days past; it is amusing to see them running about with a surprising quickness, watching our motions, and particularly our eyes.

July 2. A beautiful day for Labrador. Drew another Puffin. Went on shore, and was most pleased with what I saw. The country, so wild and grand, is of itself enough to interest any one in its wonderful dreariness. Its mossy, grey-clothed rocks, heaped and thrown together as if by chance, in the most fantastical groups imaginable, huge masses hanging on minor ones as if about to roll themselves down from their doubtful-looking situations, into the depths of the sea beneath. Bays without end, sprinkled with rocky islands of all shapes and sizes, where in every fissure a Guillemot, a Cormorant or some other wild bird retreats to secure its egg and raise its young, or save itself from the hunter.

I watched the Ring Plover for some time; the parents were so intent on saving their young that they both lay on the rocks as if shot, quivering their wings and dragging their bodies as if quite disabled. We left them and their young to the care of the Creator. I would not have shot one of the old ones, or taken one of the young for any consideration.

July 3. I had the pleasure of coming upon a Cormorant's nest [see pages 144-145], that lay in a declivity not more than four or five yards

Audubon was pleased with the "sonorous note" of the snow bunting. This one pauses en route to its nest with a meal for its young.

On one island Audubon found Atlantic puffins "breeding in great numbers", in long burrows that ran like tunnels in every direction.

below me. The mother bird was on her nest with three young; I was un-observed by her for some minutes, and was delighted to see how kindly attentive she was to her dear brood. Suddenly her keen eye saw me, and she flew off as if to dive into the sea.

July 4. At four this morning I sent Tom Lincoln on shore after four plants and a Cormorant's nest for me to draw. The nest was literally pasted to the rock's edge, so thick was the decomposed, putrid matter below it, and to which the upper part of the nest was attached. It was formed of such sticks as the country affords, sea-moss and other garbage, and weighed over fifteen pounds.

July 5. John and Lincoln returned at sunset with a Red-necked Diver, and one egg of that bird. They brought some curious Eels, and an Arctic Tern, and saw the tracks of Deer and Caribou, also Otter paths from one pond to another. They saw several Loons and *tolled* them by running towards them hallooing and waving a handkerchief, at which sight and cry the Loons immediately swam towards them, until within twenty yards. This "tolling" is curious and wonderful. Many other species of water-fowl are deceived by these maneuvers, but none so completely as the Loon.

I drew from four o'clock this morning till three this afternoon; finished a figure of the Red-necked Diver. Feeling the want of exercise, went off with the captain a few miles, to a large rough island. This afternoon I thought the country looked more terrifyingly wild than ever; the dark clouds, casting their shadows on the stupendous masses of rugged rock, lead the imagination into regions impossible to describe.

The Scoter Ducks, of which I have seen many this day, were partially moulted, and could fly only a short distance, and must be either barren or the young bachelors, as I find *parents* in full plumage. I have ob-served this strange fact so often now that I shall say no more about it; I have found it in nearly all the species of the birds here. I do not know of any writer on the history of birds having observed this curious fact.

July 6. John found the nest of a White-crowned Bunting with five eggs; he was creeping through some low bushes after a Red-necked Diver, and accidentally coming upon it, startled the female, which made much noise and complaint. The nest was placed in the moss, under a low bough, and formed of beautiful moss outwardly, dried, fine grass next inside, and exquisitely lined with fibrous roots of a rich yellow colour; the eggs are light greenish, slightly sprinkled with reddish-brown, in size about the same as eggs of the Song Sparrow.

July 8. Rainy, dirty weather, wind east. The rain falls on my drawing-paper, in spite of all I can do, and even the fog collects and falls in large drops from the rigging of my table; now and again I am obliged to close my skylight, and then may be said to work almost in darkness. Notwithstanding, I finished my cock Ptarmigan, and three more young, and now consider it a handsome large plate [see pages 142-143].

July 10. Could I describe one of these dismal gales which blow ever and anon over this desolate country, it would in all probability be of interest to one unacquainted with the inclemency of the climate. Nowhere else is the power of the northeast gale, which blows every week on the coast of Labrador, so keenly felt as here. I cannot describe it; all I can say is that while we are in as fine and safe a harbor as could be wished for, and completely land-locked all round, so strong does the wind blow, and so great its influence on our vessel, that her motion will not allow me to draw, and indeed once this day forced me to my berth, as well as some others of our party. One would imagine all the powers of Boreas had been put to work to give us a true idea of what his energies can produce, even in so snug a harbor. What is felt outside I cannot imagine, but greatly fear that few vessels could ride safely before these horrid blasts, that now and then seem strong enough to rend the very rocks asunder. The rain is driven in sheets which seem scarcely to fall on sea or land; I can hardly call it rain, it is rather a mass of water, so thick that all objects at any distance are lost to sight every three or four minutes, and the waters comb up and beat about us in our rock-bound harbor as a newly caged bird does against its imprisoning walls.

The Great Black-backed Gull alone is seen floating through the storm, screaming loudly and mournfully as it seeks its prey; not another bird is to be seen abroad; the Cormorants are all settled in the rocks close to us, the Guillemots are deep in the fissures, every Eider Duck hides under the lee of some point, her brood snugly beneath her opened wings; the Loon and the Diver have crawled among the rankest weeds, and are patiently waiting for a return of fair weather; the Grouse is quite hidden under the creeping willow; the Great Grey Owl is perched on the southern declivity of some stupendous rock.

July 11. The gale, or hurricane, or whatever else the weather of yesterday was, subsided about midnight, and at sunrise this morning it was quite calm, and the horizon fiery red. It soon became cloudy, and the wind has been all round the compass.

July 12. I saw a Black-backed Gull plunge on a Crab as big as my two fists, in about two feet of water, seize it and haul it ashore, where it ate it while I watched; I could see the Crab torn piece by piece, until the shell and legs alone remained. The Gull then flew in a direct line towards her nest about a mile distant, probably to disgorge her food in favour of her young.

Our two young Gulls, which we now have had for nearly a month, act just as Vultures would. We throw them a dead Duck or even a dead Gull, and they tear it to pieces, drinking the blood and swallowing the flesh, each constantly trying to rob the other of the piece of flesh which he has torn from the carcass. They do not drink water, but frequently wash the blood off their bills by plunging them into water, and then violently shaking their heads. They are now half fledged.

July 14. [In Little Mecatina Harbor.] Our harbor is the very representation of the bottom of a large bowl, in the centre of which our vessel is safely at anchor, surrounded by rocks fully a thousand feet high, and the wildest-looking place I ever was in.

July 17. The mosquitoes so annoyed me last night that I did not even close my eyes. I tried the deck of the vessel, and although the fog was as thick as fine rain, these insects attacked me by thousands, and I returned below, where I continued fighting them until daylight, when I had a roaring fire made and got rid of them. The fog has been as thick as ever, and rain has fallen heavily, although the wind is south-west.

July 18. We found a nest of the Hudson's Bay Titmouse, containing four young able to fly; we procured the parents also, and I shall have the pleasure of sketching them tomorrow; to my knowledge this bird has never been drawn. Their *manners* resemble those of the Black-headed Titmouse, or Chickadee, and their notes are fully as strong and clamorous, and constant as those of either of our own species. The nest was dug by the bird out of a dead and rotten stump, about five feet from the ground; the aperture, one-and-a-quarter inches in diameter, was as round as if made by a small Woodpecker, or a Flying-squirrel. The hole inside was four by six inches; at the bottom a bed of chips was found; the nest itself resembled a purse formed of the most beautiful and softest hair imaginable—of Sables, Ermines, Martens, Hares, etc.; a warmer and snugger apartment no bird could desire.

July 21. I write now from a harbor which has no name, for we have mistaken it for the right one, which lies two miles east of this; but it matters little, for the coast of Labrador is all alike: comfortless, cold and foggy, yet grand.

July 22. This afternoon the wind has been blowing a tremendous gale; our anchors have dragged with sixty fathoms of chain out. Crows are not abundant here; the Ravens equal them in number, and Peregrine

A fast-moving gale sweeps down the Labrador coast at Cape Makkovik. Audubon was continually awed by such sudden storms.

Falcons are more numerous. The horseflies are so bad that they drove our young men on board.

July 23. We have had a fine day, but very windy. The Caribou flies have driven the hunters back on board; Tom Lincoln, who is especially attacked by them, was covered with blood, and looked as if he had had a gouging fight with some rough Kentuckians. The mosquitoes trouble me so much that in driving them away I bespatter my paper with ink.

July 24. The Semi-palmated Plover breeds on the tops or sides of the high hills, and amid the moss of this country. I have not found a nest, but have been so very near the spot where one undoubtedly was, that the female has moved before me, trailing her wings and spreading her tail to draw me away; uttering a plaintive note, the purpose of which I easily conceive. The Shore Lark has served us the same way; that nests must also be placed amid the deep mosses, over which these beautiful birds run as nimbly as can be imagined. They have the power of giving two notes, so very different from each other that a person not seeing the bird would be inclined to believe that two birds of different species were at hand. Often after these notes comes a sweet trill; all these I have thought were in intimation of danger, and with the wish to induce the sitting mate to lie quiet and silent.

July 26. I did not write last night because we were at sea and the motion was too disagreeable, and my mind was as troubled as the ocean. We left our harbor before five in the morning, with a good breeze. At daylight we found ourselves at the mouth of Bras d'Or [Bradore] harbor, where we are snugly moored.

The snow is still to be seen in patches on every hill around us; the borders of the water courses are edged with grasses and weeds as rank of growth as may be seen in the Middle States in like situations. I saw a small brook filled with fine trout; but what pleased me best, I found a nest of the Shore Lark; it was embedded in moss so much the colour of the birds, that when these sit on it, it is next to impossible to observe them; it was buried to its full depth, about seven inches—composed outwardly of mosses of different sorts; within, fine grass circularly arranged, and mixed with many large, soft Duck feathers. These birds breed on high table-lands, one pair to a certain district. The place where I found the nest was so arid, poor and rocky that nothing grew there. We see the high mountains of Newfoundland, the summits, at present, far above the clouds.

July 28. Breakfast over, we proceeded over the table-lands towards some ponds. I found three young Shore Larks just out of the nest, and not yet able to fly; they hopped pretty briskly over the moss; uttering a soft *peep*, to which the parent bird responded at every call. I am glad that it is in my power to make a drawing of these birds in summer, winter, and young plumage.

July 29. "The Curlews are coming"; this is as much of a saying here as that about the Wild Pigeons in Kentucky. It is now calm, for a wonder, but as cold as vengeance, on deck; we have a good fire in the stove, and I am roasting on one side and freezing on the other.

July 30. It was a beautiful morning when I arose, and such a thing as a beautiful morning in this mournful country almost amounts to a phenomenon. The captain and myself went off to an island and searched for a Horned Lark and found a good number of old and young, associated, both equally wild. The young were led off with great care by the adults, and urged to squat quietly until nearly within gunshot, when at a "tweet" from the parent they took to the wing and were off.

August 4. This species of Curlew, the smallest I have ever seen, feeds on the berries it procures, with a rapidity equalled only by that of the Passenger Pigeon; in an instant all the ripe berries on the plant are plucked and swallowed, and the whole country is cleared of these berries. In their evolutions they resemble Pigeons also, sweeping over the ground, cutting backwards and forwards, and now and then poising in the air like a Hawk in sight of quarry.

The fruits are now ripe, yet six weeks ago the whole country was a sheet of snow, the bays locked in ice, the air a constant storm. Now the grass is rich in growth, at every step flowers are met with, insects fill the air, the snow-banks are melting; now and then an appearance as of summer does exist, but in thirty days all is over; the dark northern clouds will enwrap the mountain summits; the rivulets, the ponds, the rivers, the bays themselves will begin to freeze; snowfalls will cover all these shores, and nature will resume her sleeping state, nay, more than that, one of desolation and death. Wonderful! Wonderful! But this marvellous country must be left to an abler pen than mine to describe.

Audubon's "Feathered Musicians"

Eloquent as Audubon was in the journal of his expedition (previous pages), his most impressive tribute to Labrador was the pictorial record he brought back.

By 1833, when he chartered the schooner *Ripley* for his trip, John James Audubon was already a generation ahead of his contemporaries in the skill with which he portrayed America's birdlife. He had taken up this career almost by accident. The bastard son of a French naval captain and a governess, he was born in Haiti in 1785 and adopted by his father and the captain's forgiving wife. Baptized in France as Jean Jacques Fougère Audubon, he went to America at 18, evidently to escape Napoleon's conscription. He became a tradesman and property speculator on the American frontier, only to be made bankrupt and jailed for debt in the land panic of 1819. Released from prison, he turned to two hobbies—painting and bird-watching—combined them and soon became internationally famous.

Audubon pursued his feathered subjects down the Mississippi to Louisiana and the Florida Keys, and west to Texas. He was 48 when he sailed north to Labrador to study the birds in their mating plumage.

As indefatigable as ever, Audubon worked from before dawn until after dark day after day during his Labrador expedition. While his English-born wife Lucy stayed behind in Boston, he took along his son John, who helped complete some of his father's paintings and did some bird portraits of his own. Audubon, his son and his assistants aboard *Ripley* saw more birds than they could count, including some they had never seen before, and some that were even endangered. Within a generation, at least two of these species—the great auk and the Labrador duck—were extinct.

Audubon never ceased to marvel at the phenomenon of birds migrating to Labrador's seemingly inhospitable coast. "That the Creator," he wrote, "should have commanded millions of delicate, diminutive, tender creatures to cross immense spaces of country to all appearance a thousand times more congenial to them than this, to cause them to people, as it were, this desolate land for a time, to enliven it by the songs of the sweet feathered musicians for two months at most, and by the same command induce them to abandon it, almost suddenly, is as wonderful as it is beautiful."

Along the coast of Labrador, Audubon saw numerous gyrfalcons (Falco rusticolus) like the quarrelling adults on the right. In his journal he observed that the flight of this handsome predator "resembled that of the Peregrine Falcon, but was more elevated, majestic and rapid". Hovering high over their prey, Audubon noted, gyrfalcons "would descend almost perpendicularly on their unsuspecting victims".

Scouting for birds ashore, Audubon found these Lincoln's sparrows (Melospiza lincolnii)—a "petulant and pugnacious" species, he called them—on June 27, 1833. "I found it to be a species which I had not previously seen," Audubon wrote in his journal, and "named it Tom's Finch", in honour of one of his assistants, Tom Lincoln.

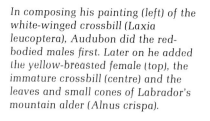

In composing his painting (left) of the white-winged crossbill (Laxia leucoptera), Audubon did the red-bodied males first. Later on he added the yellow-breasted female (top), the immature crossbill (centre) and the leaves and small cones of Labrador's mountain alder (Alnus crispa).

Early on the morning of July 18, in Labrador's coastal marshes, Audubon spotted some boreal chickadees (Parus hudsonicus) and sketched them, completing the painting (above) aboard Ripley two days later. The fruit on which they are feeding is black chokeberry (Aronia melanocarpa).

One special reason for Audubon's
expedition was to pursue the red-
throated loon (Gavia stellata). By
mid-May these birds had flown north
from the latitude of Boston; and to
"study their habits at this season",
Audubon explained, "we must follow
them to the islands in the mouth of the
broad St. Lawrence, or the granitic rocks
of Labrador". He found these loons on
the coast in July and painted the two
adults (in the water) in breeding
plumage beside one chick. The loon
in winter plumage (left) apparently
was added to the painting later.

"On the high and desolate tracts of Labrador," Audubon reported how he traced the horned lark (Eremophila alpestris). He drew three chicks at their

On July 6 Audubon came upon this family of willow ptarmigan (Lagopus lagopus), the male standing guard.

nest (left), then added "a beautiful male in full summer plumage" (centre). The other two specimens were incorporated from a drawing made earlier.

"I still see the high rolling billows of the St. Lawrence breaking in foaming masses against the huge Labrador cliffs where the Cormorant places its nest on the shelves," Audubon wrote. "I lay flat on the edge of a precipice, a hundred feet above the turbulent waters." He decided not to disturb the birds, but later his assistants brought him a nest and some chicks so that he could do this portrait of a family of cormorants (Phalacrocorax carbo).

On a rocky beach Audubon painted a male surf scoter (Melanitta perspicillata) (left) and female feeding on clams.

Audubon spent an entire day in mid-June drawing these adult razorbills (Alca torda) in their spring plumage.

"I observed Puffins (Fratercula arctica) every day," Audubon noted. He showed these two in their spring plumage.

The pomarine jaeger (Stercorarius pomarinus) was elusive; but some assistants finally captured this one for Audubon.

After a stormy day alongside Gannet Rock, Audubon did this painting of an adult gannet (Marus bassanus) and young (foreground).

Gannet Rock itself is in the background, swarming with the birds. Their nests, he noticed, were "in regular lines . . . like furrows".

6/ Between Forest and Tundra

The dispensation under which wild creatures more or less match their natural surroundings, at times seem part of them, is at its simplest in the north. WILLIAM B. CABOT/ LABRADOR

When you feel cold you can still concentrate on other things—the landscape around you, where you are going, what to watch for on the way. But when you feel *very* cold, you can think of practically nothing but how cold you are.

As we travelled across a frozen bay on the Labrador Sea, I was as cold as I could ever remember being. It occurred to me that perhaps, through recent years of urban living in moderately frigid Montreal, I had lost some of the tolerance to extremely low temperatures that I had when I was growing up in north-western Ontario. Or maybe advancing age was beginning to tell. Anyway, I thought I would freeze. And in fact, my nose did freeze.

Not that I was unprepared. My northern background had taught me not to trifle with sub-zero weather. I was wearing three pairs of heavy socks inside felt-lined snow boots; I also wore long thermal underwear, padded underpants, fur-lined, wind-resistant overpants, two sweaters, a scarf and a Canadian Army Arctic parka with the hood pulled tightly over a woollen toque so that only my eyes and nose were exposed. For all that, the Labrador winter got to me. When I later discovered that the bridge of my nose was frostbitten, I mentally recorded a new lesson in coping with Labrador's extremely low temperatures: don't wear steel-rimmed glasses; the metal frame conducts the heat away from your skin.

It was not only the temperature that did me in. It was a combination of low temperature and wind: the wind chill factor. The thermometer registered —28°F., and the wind was whipping across the ice and snow at 30 m.p.h. I too was whipping along at 30 m.p.h. The combination provided a wind chill factor of about —70°F. No amount of clothing can protect you completely in those conditions.

I was riding on a sled called a komatik, a versatile vehicle that is a tribute to the endless ingenuity of the Eskimo. This Arctic dogsled consists of long steel-shod wooden runners intricately stitched with rope to a succession of boards that make up the carrying surface. The komatik is as flexible as a snake, fluidly hugging the contours of the snow-covered land as you glide uphill and down. Originally it was pulled by a dog team; but progress has reached even northern Labrador in the form of the motor-driven snowmobile, which moves faster and more efficiently—meanwhile assaulting the white, silent wilderness with its noise. My komatik was pulled by such a snowmobile.

One of its disadvantages, I found, was that it moved *too* fast. When you are riding behind a dog team, you can warm yourself from time to time by jumping off the komatik and running alongside. But when you ride a fast-moving komatik being pulled by an inexhaustible engine, the speed is such that you have to sit there and suffer, holding on with hands aching from the cold in spite of your elbow-length windproof gauntlets and knitted inner mitts.

So I was glad to get off. My guide and driver, an exceptionally capable 16-year-old named Bernard Webb, had pulled off the ice of the bay and halted half-way up a little valley. I rose stiffly from my frozen seat of wolf skins and launched into the traditional northern warm-up dance that looks so ridiculous but is nevertheless so essential in Labrador's winter weather; jogging on the spot, flapping my arms and beating my hands together to restore circulation. Little by little I could feel the warm blood flowing back into extremities that had lost their normal supply of body heat.

While bouncing up and down, I looked at Bernard enviously. He was dressed much more effectively than I was, in a pull-over Eskimo parka called a dickie, with another parka made of felt-like duffle cloth underneath. I particularly admired his sealskin boots, which were made by his mother; nothing has ever matched the original Eskimo clothing as a defence against Labrador's cold. Still, he looked cold too; a patch of frost clung to one cheek where his breath had blown back on his face and frozen. He pointed at a snow-and-lichen-covered patch of rock with a chunk of meat from the belly of a porcupine sitting on it. "One of my brother Bill's traps," he said. "Thought you might like to stop and take a look at it. Might have been a fox in it; you never know."

"Red or Arctic fox?" I asked.

"Both kinds. They hang around the same places. They hate each other, though."

"Ever actually see them together in the same place?"

"Oh sure. Right now there's a grounded whale on a bay just up beyond here—it must be 30 feet long. The red foxes and white foxes are both feeding off it. The other day one of the boys goes up there, and there's this red fox and white fox fighting, really going at it, paying no attention to him. He shoots the red one but the white one just keeps on fighting the red one's dead body. So then he shoots the white one, too."

As we hit the trail again, I reflected that Bernard's story uniquely exemplified the area we were entering. The southern part of Labrador is composed mostly of forest area. The northern part is treeless tundra. But the forest does not end abruptly, with a row of trees edging the open tundra. Instead, there is a marginal area with fewer and fewer trees. It gradually phases into the tundra with its rolling plains of caribou moss, sedges and willow bushes that can survive on the almost permanently frozen ground called permafrost.

This transitional belt does not cut a straight line of division across the continent, but varies widely in latitude, depending on local climatic conditions. Often it consists of a patchwork of forest and barren land. But gradually, as you go north, the land becomes more and more barren, until finally you are in bare subarctic tundra.

Tundra to the north, forest to the south; and a meandering section between them, where each ecosystem phases into the other. In the south the type of forest is termed "mixed"; although coniferous trees predominate, there are plenty of deciduous trees. I recall, on my first visit to Labrador, being surprised by the forests of the southern area. I was prepared by what I had read to find all of Labrador a barren "land God gave to Cain". But the first time I travelled up the Churchill River from Goose Bay I saw stands of pure white birch and stately quaking aspens as fine as I had seen anywhere. Among them were scattered specimens of mountain ash, along with non-deciduous white spruces and balsam firs that grow best in more temperate climates. Only after I had been there a while did I start to notice the differences. As autumn advanced, there were no bold crimson splashes of dying maple leaves amid the delicate bronze and silver of the birch and aspen leaves. The familiar jack pine was missing, and so were other varieties. There was no white pine, no cedar, no hemlock, no black ash.

Then something else struck me: I had been there for more than a week and I hadn't seen a single chipmunk. Nor were there any of the blue jays or red-winged blackbirds one would expect to see around a camp if it were located farther south. I also learned from the local people that there were no racoons and skunks—no snakes or rats, either. When the people talked about "deer", they did not mean white-tailed deer; there aren't any at all here. In local parlance "deer" are caribou. The trappers had never heard of the sable-like animal called a fisher. Clearly this was considerably different from the Canadian forest I had known in my boyhood.

Then, as I travelled farther north, it became more different still. The deciduous trees disappeared; instead there were groves where black spruce grew in patches much farther apart from one another than most trees in the Canadian bush. Lone tamaracks, always inexplicably leaning to the east, filled the gaps between the black spruces. This was what the botanists call boreal woodland, to distinguish it from the dense and disorderly boreal forest of the more southerly regions of Canada. The woodland begins where the first permafrost underlies the soil. It looks almost like a park on an English country estate.

This land beyond the boreal forest is also called "taiga" (a word borrowed from Siberia, as is "tundra"). As you move through it you can see the law of the survival of the fittest at work, in the botanical sense. The land's most distinctive feature is the greenish-white caribou moss that grows on this rocky, acid soil. The aridity of the soil permits little other vegetation. Caribou moss is misnamed; it is not really a moss, but a peculiarly hardy form of lichen. The stuff is soft but strong enough so that it can be cut to make a nappy for an Indian baby, and even absorbent enough to be used as a lamp wick. Because it contains carbohydrates, the Eskimos mix it with seal meat to feed their dogs and vary the dogs' high-protein diet. When caribou moss is moist on a hot day, it is delightful to walk on barefooted. When it is dry, it is dangerous: it turns to perfect tinder for forest fires. As the name implies, the moss is the staff of life for the vast herds of caribou that roam Labrador.

The caribou moss might seem at first to support the trees of the taiga, but in the long run it does the opposite. As it piles up, it tends to keep the trees' seeds from reaching the soil, where they can take root. This explains why the black spruce is by far the most prevalent tree in Labrador. The black spruce has an alternative method of reproduction.

In the absence of places to spread its seeds, its lower branches develop independent roots that may eventually establish each branch as a tree in its own right. A black spruce with baby trees growing from its branches is called a candelabrum spruce, and it does indeed look like a candelabrum. Black spruce have shallow roots; and when an old tree topples over, the new trees on the branches send their own roots down into the soil and soon become established in their own right.

Foresters have an enormous respect for this homely tree, which better than any other wages the fight for survival in the north. In areas where its seeds can easily reach the ground, the spruce grows straight and thin, with few branches for much of its length. Many such specimens have a clump of brush right at the top, as if their growing power were concentrated on reaching maximum height. But black spruce always make the most of the growing opportunities that are available. In southern Labrador I have seen them standing like church spires at more than 90 feet. I have also seen mature black spruces stunted by cold weather in the tundra regions, and no higher than my waist. Cut down one of these shrub-like growths and count its tight age rings, and you may find that it is more than 100 years old.

Black spruce trees graphically illustrate how the taiga almost grudgingly gives way to the tundra. Bernard Webb and I were headed north towards Webb Bay, where Bernard's great-grandfather had built the family's first cabin. As I looked at the trees on the hills around us, I was reminded of an army advancing uphill against overwhelming opposition. At the bases of the mountainsides there were masses of spruces, interspersed with tamaracks. The tamarack, a species of larch, is an immensely tough tree; but even where the tamaracks could no longer grow on the bald rock, there were still numerous black spruces. Up they went, their ranks thinning as the slope of the Precambrian rock became more exposed. Like soldiers under intense fire, the trees crouched closer to the ground the higher they climbed. Soon there was a cluster of just three trees, each bent almost double, separated by a few paces. And a few paces ahead of these, half-way up the mountain, was the last of the black spruces—stunted, tattered and ugly, but still clinging to its hard, frozen foothold.

Bernard, too, was looking at trees—the ones at the lower levels. He stopped again and sprang off the snowmobile, unslinging his rifle and dashing off into the brush. He had spotted some tracks made by spruce grouse, which often live under the trees. Not only do they shelter there; they also eat the seeds and needles, blighting the trees' regeneration.

In a vivid example of the no-man's land that lies between Labrador's forest and tundra, a last black spruce (foreground) holds out against the harsh winds on a hill near Webb Bay. North of this hill is treeless tundra, sustaining only sedges and other ground-hugging growth.

It is all part of the competition for a livelihood in this sparse land, with one living thing always feeding off another. Nothing is exempt—not the trees, not even the rock. The lichens produce acid that eats into the rock, in a process that eventually breaks the rock into rubble.

One of the rarest competitors in the struggle for survival in this northern part of Labrador is the only primate to inhabit the country: *Homo sapiens*. Bernard was not hunting grouse for the fun of it, but because the members of his family, in their solitary home in the wilderness, must depend on wild things for most of their food supply. Bernard had explained to me why his great-grandfather had selected this ecological no-man's land for his cabin site and why the Webb family had lived there ever since. They make their livelihood by trapping, hunting and fishing; and the area around the bay offers a rich variety of fauna from the two ecological systems. There are Arctic hares of the tundra and snowshoe hares of the forest, ptarmigan of the north and spruce grouse of the south, Arctic char and southern lake trout. For a family living off the land, the location offers the best of the two worlds. They live off a country that does not permit agriculture but will yield an amazing variety of useful things for the ingenious inhabitant: sealskin boots, caribou skin sleeping bags, hand-carved wooden toys for the children— plus almost all the family's foodstuffs. Bernard's mother and father have raised a family of 11 this way.

But it could scarcely be called an easy life. In fact, it is hard and at times dangerous. In 1911 the British explorer H. Hesketh Prichard, the same visitor who was so tormented by Labrador's mosquitoes (Chapter 4), wrote that all life in Labrador, including human life, is entirely predatory. He exaggerated a little, since there are plenty of herbivores. But he wasn't too far wrong. Since his analysis, an air base has been built at Goose Bay; iron mines have been opened in western Labrador; a hydro-electric project serving Quebec Province has been constructed at Churchill Falls. These projects have altered Labrador's natural law of survival somewhat, but not so much as an outsider might think. The lives of traditional Labradorians—Eskimo, Indian, white or in-between —are still tightly tied to the natural order of things. Life here largely remains that of the hunter and the hunted.

The human hunter has some advantages, to be sure, over the wild creatures of Labrador. Yet, in spite of the efficiency of firearms, sophisticated fishing equipment and mechanized transport, life from day to day is still hazardous. I was standing on the dock in Nain chatting with a schoolteacher one autumn day when a Canadian Armed Forces search-rescue aircraft flew over us, heading north. "They're looking for an Eskimo family that's lost up the coast," the teacher told me. "They went up fishing. A man and his wife and two children." They were never seen again.

After bumping along on the komatik for upwards of four hours, I had begun to realize more keenly than ever before that man's most relentless enemy up here is the cold, especially when one is hungry, as I was. Hunger sharply reduces one's resistance to the cold because the body burns off so many calories in the process of keeping warm. I reflected that there must be few, if any, vegetarians among the people of Labrador. Exposure causes a craving for meat, especially fat. When you have insufficient protein, you become vulnerable to a condition known as hypothermia; it occurs when the body loses more heat than it generates. The symptoms are extreme fatigue, dizziness and loss of balance.

But, as the old-timers like to say, it can always get colder. And so it did, as Bernard accelerated the snowmobile to its top speed and the wind flayed my face like a lash. Then I looked around and saw another snowmobile with its komatik, far across the ice.

It, too, was going flat out. My first reaction was: the crazy fools are racing! But then I saw Bernard tear off his mitts and unsling his rifle. I realized what was happening. The other snowmobile was chasing a big grey wolf that was running diagonally across the ice. Bernard was trying to head it off.

The wolf, already wounded, was leaving a trickle of blood on the ice, but that didn't slow it down. Top speed for a wolf is supposed to be 28 miles an hour, but this particular wolf didn't seem to be aware of that. It was outdistancing the other snowmobile, which must have been going at 40 m.p.h. Now Bernard was cutting across the wolf's line of retreat. He squeezed off a couple of diverting shots. The wolf broke its long stride just perceptibly, and veered towards its other pursuer, who then shot it from about 100 feet away. The wolf crashed to the ice.

We skidded to a stop and walked over to meet the man on the other snowmobile, who by then was standing close—but not too close—to the fallen animal. He turned out to be Bernard's brother Bill, who had spotted a group of three or four wolves as he rounded a point, and had managed to get a shot off and hit this one. After a minute or so Bill carefully prodded the wolf with his rifle barrel to make sure it was dead. It was. He pointed down at its mouth. The nose and mouth were bristling with porcupine quills.

This was one unlucky wolf. It had had the misfortune to run into the only two types of creature in the woods with the means to kill it. More often than not, wolves and other animals die when they suffer a dose of quills administered with a sharp slap of a porcupine's tail. A mature porcupine carries an estimated 30,000 of these barbed quills, which range in length from an inch to two inches. The quills work their way through a victim's flesh. Presumably some of the quills in this wolf's mouth would ultimately have worked their way into its brain. But the wolf probably would have died of starvation first; an animal with porcupine quills in its mouth is unable to eat. This wolf had been spared a more hideous death by being shot.

Men do not always hunt wolves solely for their fur. It is true that the fur is warm and resistant to frost, and thus makes good trim for parka hoods. But Bill explained that in this case there was a more important reason. Wolves had lately become a menace in the area. Many had stayed behind when the caribou migration had come through the year before. The wolves were now taking a heavy toll of small game and had been tearing apart animals in the Webb family's traps. Generally speaking, Bill said, the only way to kill wolves is to shoot them. It is no use trying to trap them. I recalled what another Labrador trapper once said to me: "You never gets one of them beggars in a trap. The old wolf, he's too cute to get caught."

Except for its encounters with porcupines and men, the wolf is king of the beasts in wild Labrador. Huge polar bears have been reported killed by wolf packs. Attacking in packs is one of the secrets of the wolf's success. Another is its endurance and determination. Although I was impressed with the speed of this wolf when it went tearing across the ice, a wolf is not a speedy animal in comparison with most of its prey. A healthy, mature caribou, for instance, can run at 50 miles an hour. A wolf's "cruising speed", as it were, is only five miles an hour, but it moves with a loose and easy gait that enables it to lope behind a herd of caribou for mile after mile, hour after hour. When one of the herd finally falters, the wolves in a pack put on a burst of speed to come in for the kill. Their tactical sense would do credit to a general. They out-flank their victim, taking advantage of the terrain to steer the prey into ravines where there is no escape.

The wolf the Webb boys shot was not, according to them, a very big one. It was probably from a litter of the previous year. It looked as if it weighed close to a hundred pounds, so it would have been considered a fairly large timber wolf in other parts of Canada. But the blue-grey

A lean and hungry wolf bites into the marrow of a bone it has already picked clean. The blue-grey Labrador wolf (Canus labradorius) is a canny predator, hunting its prey in packs and cleverly avoiding the traps set for it by Homo sapiens labradorius.

Canus labradorius, the subspecies of this region of Labrador, is bigger than most—it weighs 150 pounds or more when fully grown.

I looked up from this wolf and saw a stream of smoke rising straight up in the air, as it always does on cold, still days. We were not far from the Webb cabin. Here at last I was able to peel off a few layers of clothing and have a welcome "warm-up" of hot tea beside a glowing stove. Chesley Webb, the father of the family, proved to be a walking encyclopaedia of lore and legend about wolves and Labrador's other fur-bearing fauna.

Like the wolf his sons had just shot, many tundra animals are stockier and larger than their southern counterparts. An Arctic hare, for example, can reach 10 pounds—four times the weight of the southern cottontail rabbit. A polar bear, at 1,600 pounds, is five times heavier than the average black bear. Apparently, Mr. Webb explained, the larger and chunkier bodies generate more heat and radiate less of it in proportion to size than the skinnier southern animals. But equally significant is the thickness of fur—in fact, so much so that the tundra animals that are exceptions to the rule of size evidently make up for it with exceptionally thick fur. Chesley Webb went over to the wall of the cabin and took down two pelts.

"This one here," he said, handing me a creamy-white pelt, "is an Arctic fox. It's smaller than this one." He handed me the other skin, a pelt of the southern red fox.

"Feel the difference," he said. The smaller white pelt was noticeably thicker than the larger one. Running my fingers through the dense white hair, I could feel the luxuriant undercoat beneath it.

"And there's a layer of fat under that," Mr. Webb reminded me. "An Arctic fox can stand still for hours at 40 below. They look fatter, too. Sometimes you can see 'em sitting on the bluffs, yapping like little dogs. They aren't afraid of us like most of the other animals are."

When spring comes to the tundra, Chesley Webb pointed out, the Arctic fox's white fur moults, to be replaced by a brown summer coat that is much lighter. In autumn it gradually turns white again.

Labrador's white Arctic foxes are expert hunters of lemmings and voles. According to Chesley Webb, a fox on the prowl for one of these subterranean creatures is quite a sight. "He'll pad along over the snow with those broad feet, his head down, sniffing and listening. There's not a track in the snow 'cept his own. The lemmings and voles are underground in their little tunnels. Suddenly that fox will rear up and start digging in the snow. He digs just like a dog, but a lot faster than any dog I ever saw. Usually he digs down through three or four feet of snow so fast that the lemming doesn't even have time to run away through his tunnel. Fastest digger you ever saw."

Arctic foxes also prey on Arctic hares, when they can catch them, and on the snowshoe hares that live here, far from their usual forest habitat. They stalk grouse and ptarmigan. And up on the ice-bound northern tip of Labrador they follow the polar bears around on the ice floes, making meals of the seal carrion that the bears leave behind. The foxes are strong swimmers, capable of trailing after polar bears in the icy water for several miles. Although the foxes always keep a respectable distance from their huge benefactors, there is evidence that the bears and foxes have arrived at a *modus vivendi* through regular contact. They have been seen sleeping not far apart on floating ice pans.

Not all of the animals that share their food with the Arctic fox are so tolerant of it. The fox's taste for caribou carrion brings it into confrontations with wolves. Usually an Arctic fox is too quick for a wolf. But for all its speed, the Arctic fox meets its match when it confronts its southern counterpart, the red fox. As agile as the Arctic fox, the red fox is stronger. It will chase and kill a white fox when given the chance.

The red fox shares an indispensable attribute with some other creatures that have mastered this harsh northern environment—the wolf, the raven and the wolverine. That attribute is intelligence. The most intelligent beast of them all is the wolverine. This animal's natural range extends from mid-northern Canada as far north as it is possible to get on the Canadian land mass; yet in winter it does not turn white or resort to any special sheltering arrangements. In fact, it is the only northern mammal whose fur turns *darker* in winter, and it rarely takes any kind of shelter, even in the worst snowstorms. If the wolf and fox are legends in more civilized places, the wolverine is the legend of the north. Some Labradorians claim it has supernatural gifts. In any case, the wolverine is certainly an example of nature at its most efficient.

"A wolverine is a nasty old thing," Mrs. Chesley Webb said. Indeed it is. It looks nasty, smells nasty and has some very nasty habits. This overpowering nastiness is what makes it the most unpopular animal in the forest and on the tundra. Although the wolverine weighs little more than 40 pounds, its relentless ferocity is complemented by a tremendous range of natural faculties. It has prodigious endurance, prowling day and night with hardly a let-up for distances of up to 80 miles in a 24-hour period. Its feet are so large that its tracks could be mistaken for

The lonely limbo between forest and tundra is a battleground for the Arctic fox (above) and its southern counterpart, the red fox (right). The latter has gradually adapted to the Arctic fox's environment and has increasingly penetrated its territory.

those of a wolf, except that the wolverine's fifth toe is set higher and usually makes no imprint. The wolverine moves slowly, with a rolling gait suited to its stocky build, but it can be lightning fast when it springs on its prey—fast enough to catch a snowshoe hare. It is an accomplished tree climber, waiting on branches to pounce on its quarry like a cougar. It is an excellent swimmer, capable of catching muskrats in the water. And it has teeth strong enough to crush a moose's leg bone.

Unlike the wolf, a lone wolverine can kill a caribou or a moose. I have talked to men who swear they have seen a solitary wolverine drive a wolf pack away from the carcass of a caribou that the wolves have killed. I have often heard stories of a wolverine driving a big black bear to flight. It is said that the fiercest bear of all, the grizzly of the northwest, is often scared off by a wolverine. I believe it. You can believe almost anything about a wolverine. An Indian once told me about seeing one sitting on its haunches and peering about with one paw shading its eyes. I took it as a quaint exaggeration—until months later I discovered a description of this habit in a zoological text book.

In spite of its name, a wolverine is not a wolf but the largest member of the weasel family. In fact, it is more like an amalgam of all of the most resourceful animals of the wilderness. Labrador people will tell you that it is more cunning than a fox, stronger than a bear, and more savage in its attack than a lynx. It is about the size of a bear cub, and its black-and-white coloration resembles that of a skunk. It also stinks worse than a skunk.

"No wolverines around here this year, thank God," Chesley Webb told me. A single wolverine can be the ruination of a trapper. "They'll steal everything out of your traps," he said. "They'll take away the traps too, sometimes, even when a big wooden stake is driven into the ground to hold a trap down."

He said that, besides eating animals that have already been trapped, wolverines learn how to steal the bait from the traps. They reach in under the tongue of a trap and spring it. Wolverines are usually too clever to be trapped themselves, but it has happened occasionally. Sir Wilfred Grenfell, who ran a medical mission in Labrador for 50 years before his death in 1940, wrote of one such time when a wolverine had become caught in two traps set side by side. The owner of the traps understandably thought the animal was dead. While he released one trap, the wolverine lay motionless. The instant the second trap was released, the wolverine bit through the man's hand and escaped.

In a rare photograph, an elusive Labrador wolverine suns itself on a rock. So furtive is this creature that while its evidence is everywhere— looted traps, stolen food, carcasses marked by its distinctive smell—few Labradorians have seen one. Weighing only about 40 pounds, the wolverine will attack a caribou or even a moose.

Oddly for a creature so well equipped by nature, wolverines are not common. They once inhabited most of Canada, but their constant battle with hunters drove them north. Even in the vast sanctuary of Labrador, where there are far fewer trappers now than there were 50 years ago, the wolverine does not flourish. There are very few left. Next to its losing war with man, the cause of the wolverine's downfall is its voracious appetite. A wolverine will attack a porcupine head-on, braving its quills to kill and eat it. Many die when the quills make it impossible for them to eat, or pierce their stomach lining. Many more wolverines die from parasites and disease-carrying microbes contained in the rotted meat they readily consume.

In this barren area above the forest, and in the open tundra to the north, the other fauna have adapted, each in its own sometimes remarkable way. The weasel, for example, not only turns white in winter; each white hair is a hollow tube, thereby applying the insulating principle of dead air in innumerable tiny hairs all over its body. The polar bear has a double coat of thick hair over its heavy layer of fat; it also has a thick insulating wad of fur on each foot. And the polar bear's eyesight is much keener than that of the myopic southerly black bear; since the polar bear requires more protein for protection against the extreme cold, it needs keen eyes to spot the well-camouflaged—and protein-rich— seals and whale calves on which it feeds.

These differences between the northern and southern creatures are a familiar topic of conversation among the few people who inhabit the taiga. I noticed, for example, that an Arctic hare usually stands on its haunches to study a near-by human—something a snowshoe hare rarely pauses long enough to do. The local people offer a simple explanation for this: the Arctic hare has not developed the instinctive fear of man that has been bred into its forest counterpart; the Arctic hare has far fewer men to worry about. Trappers tell me that they sometimes find Arctic hares in their fox traps; these hares are carnivorous, and try to eat the meat in traps.

Forest species are well adapted to cope with their own habitat. But they have their limitations, which is why they are not found very far above the southern boundaries of the tundra. The ruffed grouse or partridge, as another example, prepares for winter by growing fringes of a horny substance on the sides of its feet; the broader base enables it to walk on top of the snow. But its Arctic-adapted counterpart, the ptarmigan, adjusts even more to accommodate itself to the colder temperatures of its more northerly habitat; it grows feathers over its legs and down over the soles of its feet, like heavy woollen stockings. The partridge does not turn white in winter; the ptarmigan does.

The caribou, in contrast to the white-tailed deer to the south, presents one of the best case studies of adaptation to the tundra environment in which it spends part of its migration existence. Its muzzle has more fur on it than a deer's, because it must forage through heavy snow; the deer feeds off trees, of which there are none in the tundra. The caribou's ears are short, heavily covered with fur and tucked well behind its antlers, so the ears radiate a minimum of heat. The caribou carries a thick winter coat of hairs, each of which has tiny insulating air bubbles inside. The hairs are shaped like very thin wedges, with the wider part at the top, thus creating a surface barrier that traps the warmed air next to the skin. The skin itself has a thick strip of fat under it.

A caribou's feet are unusually wide for its weight, preventing it from sinking deeply into the snow. And the feet actually change according to the seasons. In summer the edges of the hoofs wear down, so that the animal stands on a fleshy foot pad. With the coming of winter the hoofs grow longer and the pad shrinks, while the hair between the toes grows to cover the pads. The sharp hoofs also enable the animal to dig through the snow for food.

Labrador's aquatic creatures have also adapted to the special requirements of their habitat; many species migrate between northern and southern regions. The hair that plays such an essential part in adaptation to cold by the land-dwelling animals is, of course, missing on the whales, porpoises and dolphins that frequent the coastal waters of Labrador. Instead they have a layer of insulating blubber under their rubbery skins. The seals have both blubber and hair, as if they had not quite completed the transition to becoming oceanic mammals. But a seal's short, bristling hair is not redundant, especially in the ice-filled waters of Labrador. Water does not adhere to it, so it protects the seal's skin. Recent research has indicated that the snowy white coats of baby harp seals, which makes them the well-publicized victims of seal hunters' clubs on the ice floes off Labrador, enables the pups to absorb extra amounts of warming ultra-violet rays before they grow their blubber. Then, after three weeks of building up fat from their mothers' rich milk, growing from 15 to 100 pounds in the process, the young seals shed their white coats for darker pelts.

Of all Labrador's remarkable creatures, especially in the world above the forests and in the tundra, perhaps the most intriguing is the Eskimo dog. No longer wild, not completely domesticated, the Eskimo dog of Labrador is a living link with the natural wilderness. It is not a husky like the Alaska breed, imported by man from Siberia. The Labrador Eskimo dog is a descendant of the North American wolf, evolved to the point where it can be harnessed to a sled. The ancestral traits are still there. The Eskimo dog does not bark, but yips and howls like a wolf. When it beds down for the night in winter, it is a study in cold adaptation. First it fluffs up its fur to trap body heat. As it snuggles down in the snow, it squeezes its legs against its belly and flattens its small ears against its head. It tucks its nose into its chest and then flips up its bushy tail to cover its head entirely. These dogs can sleep at —50°F. and never get frostbite. If a blizzard is blowing, so much the better. They will choose a place to windward where the snow will drift over them like a huge insulating blanket.

An oft-told story in Labrador concerns a government official "from the outside" who got a ride with one of the legendary drivers who until recently carried the mail by dog team. The stranger awoke one morning to find the land covered with a flat coat of fresh snow. "We're stranded," he excitedly reported to the mailman. "The dogs have all left us." The mailman let his guest worry for a while. "They have, eh? Well, sir, I dare say we're in some trouble." Then he whistled, and a dozen dogs broke surface from the snow, shaking themselves and wagging their tails.

Eskimo dogs live mainly on seal meat and are as well adapted to their work as they are to the cold. I was with Gus Dicker, of Nain, one day when he and his friend Mark Saksagiak went to hitch up Gus's team. The dogs were quietly lying about when Mark came out of the house with the sealskin harnesses and traces. As soon as the dogs saw the gear, they jumped up—howling, yelping and falling over one another in their eagerness to be out on the ice pulling their komatik. I have never seen an aggregation so raring to go, college football teams included. Once the dogs were hitched up in the fantail configuration used in Labrador, they took off like a shot. Labradorians hitch their dogs fantail fashion because they travel mainly on open ice, and this formation spreads the weight evenly. In the more densely wooded areas of Canada the dogs are hitched single-file, so the team can snake through the forest.

After a few minutes Gus's team settled down to a steady trot. When the going is good on hard snow, Eskimo dogs can pull big loads for long distances. There is one recorded instance of a trader's team of 10 dogs

*Descendant of the wolf, and never
completely domesticated, Labrador's
sled dog is a living link with the
country's wilderness. One of a team in
Nain bays like its ancestor (above),
before being hitched to a sled for a
wild run across the ice (right).*

hauling a thousand pounds a distance of 180 miles in two-and-a-half days; they were still fresh at the end of the journey. A normal day's run for a big team of 10 dogs in good weather and ice conditions would be about 60 miles. A team's performance depends greatly on the lead dog. Like Gus's, it often is an older female that is mother or grandmother of others in the team. She keeps discipline, is accorded precedence at feeding time, and holds the team together by force of personality.

"Damn near perished one time when I didn't have a good leader," an old-time trapper told me. "Lost in real dirty weather. Now, if we'd of had a good leader, she'd of knowed the way." A good lead dog has an instinct for finding a trail in the worst snowstorms. It can pick up a trail the team may not have travelled in years, or a trail made by another team. People who have gone snowblind have often been saved through their dogs, who are immune to the affliction, finding the way home. The dogs also have a way of gauging the thickness of ice, steering clear of thin spots that are impossible for a man to detect.

But the wild wolf in them is just beneath the surface. Eskimo dogs are fearless, ready to tackle a polar bear or a wolf pack. In the latter case, the owners find it difficult to shoot because they can hardly tell the wolves and the dogs apart. And the dogs' wildness can be menacing. One night I was staying at the home of an old Indian and had to go to the outdoor privy. As I was going through the door, my host handed me a long, heavy stick. "What's that for?" I asked. He looked a little surprised. "Why, for the dogs, in case they go at you." Luckily my movements elicited only a few sleepy growls.

You can always half-expect a fight to break out among Eskimo dogs. They fly at each other frequently, and they can wind up killing one another if you don't wade into the melee swinging a stick to drive them apart. Isaac Winters, of Hopedale, told me that he has been knocked down and attacked twice while breaking up such fights. "I beat them off both times, or I wouldn't be talking to you," he said. "They go for the throat, you know." Children frequently have been maimed or killed when wandering in among a pack of Eskimo dogs. And there have been several incidents of grown men and women being killed and eaten by their own teams.

One explanation for the dogs' behaviour is that in the past they were often mistreated. It was the custom to set them loose to fend for their own food when their work was done each winter. The half-starved, marauding dogs were a dangerous nuisance around the settlements. One experimental project to raise sheep in the Nain area came to a quick end when the dogs killed all the sheep. A few years ago the Mounted Police started executing any Eskimo dog caught running loose. This policy hastened the demise of dog teams in Labrador.

But the dog sled was already becoming a thing of the past. Long-range winter transportation had been taken over by aircraft, and short-range transportation by snowmobiles. These noisy but practical machines (referred to colloquially by the leading brand name, "Ski-Doo") have replaced Eskimo dogs the way cars replaced horses elsewhere. There still are some Labradorians who stick to dogs ("You can't eat a Ski-Doo," one told me), but the few teams left are considered oddities. Once in a while you run into someone like Isaac Winters who still prefers a dog team because "they'll go where a snowmobile won't go". For the most part, though, the era of the dog team is over.

It's a little sad, considering the role the Eskimo sled dog once played in Labrador. Not only did the dog provide transportation; it also lived with its master in a mutually dependent relationship that bridged the gap between the wild things of Labrador and its human beings. Often the dogs saved the master's life; always they proved able to cope, on their own, with an environment too harsh for humans without help. With modern technology man is replacing the sled dog, and slowly—very slowly—conquering Labrador's wilderness. But, as the Eskimo dog proved daily, man in the wilderness has no monopoly on resourcefulness. The sled dog, the wild creatures, the rugged country itself, constantly remind us that humility before nature is essential to human survival—in Labrador and everywhere else.

An Armada of Ice

Like ghostly fleets of ships, icebergs are launched by the thousands every year. Creaking and booming, crashing into the sea like ships sliding down the ways, they lurch into the water, right themselves, then slowly swing with the wind and the current. Most icebergs of north-east America originate in Greenland, where glaciers still move down to the sea and, piece by gigantic piece, break off into the water.

In their pristine form these floating islands of pure ice gleam brilliantly in the sun (right), sparkling like mountains of diamonds. The analogy is apt: just as a diamond is composed of crystals of carbon, the blue-white ice is composed of crystals of H_2O. After some months at sea, when the sun has repeatedly melted its surface and it has frozen again, a berg's more granular ice presents a softer hue (following pages). But whether hard and brilliant or a snowy mass, an iceberg is an object of rare beauty, and a photographer's delight.

Most icebergs are photographed only after they have been carried by winds and currents down Baffin Bay and through Davis Strait. Rare are the pictures, such as the one opposite and the one on the next two pages, caught off Greenland during the early stage of the iceberg's odyssey. It can take as long as two years for a berg to complete its voyage south. Meanwhile it bumps ashore or strands on shallows and is locked in for the winter, then drifts with the currents when the icefields open up again in warmer weather.

During such freeze-ups the icebergs are nearly indistinguishable from the snow-covered hills along the shore. Not until the summer thaw releases them are they identifiable. Then, finally, they swing into the Labrador Current and, like a scattered ice armada, pass grandly in review down Labrador's coast.

The pictures on these pages were taken by three photographers. Most show the effects of weather and water on icebergs that have been at sea a couple of years—melted by the sun, battered by storm waves, rolling and splitting as their centres of gravity shifted and changed. The photographers have caught the surrealistic shapes, the weathered patterns and the massive majesty of these bergs as they move southwards, irresistible in their progress, to their inevitable disintegration.

Still resembling the flowing sheet of glacial ice from which it recently broke away, a newly calved iceberg glimmers as it moves out to sea near the Greenland coast. Its sheer ice surface has not yet melted under the sun and refrozen, as it will during its voyage down the Labrador Current.

After months at sea this iceberg has melted under the sun and refrozen. Its more granulated surface has taken on a softer sheen. Drifting through Baffin Bay on its way south to the Labrador Current, it passes jagged hunks of pack ice (background right) and another crevassed, fractured iceberg (left).

What looks like a mushroom is a berg that has melted and risen to expose some of its underwater proportions. The ledge was at the sea's surface.

The tortured shape of this iceberg, rising now as it melts, is caused by splitting and widening along the original glacier's fracture lines.

Reminiscent of a floating Parthenon, a disintegrating iceberg graphically illustrates the so-called "radiator effect": as fractures in the berg

were widened by melting, the exposed surfaces in the middle melted faster than the top and bottom. Wave action hastened the process.

Off the Labrador coast, a stately procession of icebergs moves through pack ice, at a time when a passing ship emphasizes their proportions. The smaller chunks are pack ice, which in winter will lock the icebergs in its grip until spring, when they will continue their voyage south to warmer waters and eventual dissolution.

Bibliography

Audubon, John James, *The Original Water-Color Paintings for The Birds of America.* Vols. 1, 2, American Heritage Publishing Co., 1966.

Audubon, Maria R., *Audubon and His Journals.* Vol. 1, Charles Scribner's Sons, 1897.

Banfield, A. W. F., *The Mammals of Canada.* Information Canada, 1974.

Banfill, B. J., *Labrador Nurse.* Charles Scribner's Sons, 1942.

Borror, Donald J. and Richard E. White, *A Field Guide to Insects.* Houghton Mifflin Company, 1970.

Britton, Nathaneal Lord and The Hon. Addison Brown, *An Illustrated Flora of The Northern United States, Canada, and The British Possessions.* New York Botanical Garden, 1936.

Brooke, C. and Robert K. Enders, *The Nature of Living Things.* The New American Library of Canada, 1964.

Bryce, George, *The Remarkable Hudson's Bay Company.* William Briggs, 1914.

Cabot, William B., *Labrador.* Small, Maynard & Co. Inc.,'1920.

Cahalane, Victor H., *Mammals of North America.* The Macmillan Co., 1947.

The Canadian Pacific Railway Company, *The Game Fishes of Canada.* 1928.

"The Churchill Falls News". Churchill Falls, Labrador.

Collins, F. H. Woodling, *The Angler's Book of Canadian Fishes.* Don Mills, 1959.

Douglas, John Scott, *The Story of The Oceans.* Dodd, Mead and Co., 1952.

Edey, Maitland A., *The Northeast Coast.* Time-Life Books, 1972-73.

Explorers Club Tales. Dodd, Mead & Co., 1936.

Foreman, J. B., *Ed., A Book of Canada.* Collins, 1962.

Fredeen, F. J. H., *Black Flies.* Information Canada, 1973.

Gillett, J. D., *Mosquitos.* Weidenfeld and Nicolson, 1971.

Godfrey, W. Earl, *The Birds of Canada.* Information Canada, 1974.

Gosling, W. G., *Labrador.* Alston Rivers, 1910.

Gosling, W. G., *Labrador, Its Discovery, Exploration and Development.* The Musson Book Co. Ltd., 1911.

Goudie, Elizabeth, and David Zimmerly, *Ed., Woman of Labrador.* Peter Martin and Associates, 1973.

Grenfell, Wilfred T., *A Labrador Doctor.* Houghton Mifflin Company, 1919.

Grenfell, Wilfred T., *The Romance of Labrador.* The Macmillan Co., 1970.

Groen, P., *The Waters of the Sea.* D. Van Norstrand, 1967.

Headstrom, Richard, *Nature in Miniature.* Alfred A. Knopf, 1968.

Heath, Douglas, *Ed.,* "Among the Deep Sea Fishers". International Grenfell Association, October, 1975.

Hosie, R. C., *Native Trees of Canada.* Information Canada, 1969.

Hubbard, Jr., Mrs. Leonidas, *A Woman's Way through Unknown Labrador.* The McClure Co., 1908.

Hylander, Clarence J. and Edith Farrington Johnston, *The Macmillan Wild Flower Book.* The Macmillan Co., 1954.

Johnston, Ken, *The Vanishing Harvest.* A Montreal Star Book, 1972.

Kerr, J. Lennox, *Wilfred Grenfell, His Life and Work.* The Ryerson Press, 1959.

Lawrence. R. D., *Wildlife in North America.* Thomas Nelson & Sons (Canada) Ltd., 1974.

Løken, O., "On the Vertical Extent of Glaciation in Northeastern Labrador—Ungava", in *Geomorphology—Selected Readings,* J. G. Nelson and M. J. Chambers, *Eds.* Methuen, 1969.

McLean, John, *Notes of a Twenty-Five Years' Service in the Hudson's Bay Territory.* London, 1849.

Merrick, Elliott, *Northern Nurse.* Charles Scribner's Sons, 1942.

Moon, Barbara, *The Canadian Shield.* N.S.L. Natural Sciences of Canada Ltd., 1970.

The Moravian Mission, *The Moravian Mission in Labrador.* 1971.

Mowat, Farley, *Westviking.* McCelland and Stewart Ltd., 1965.

Orr, Robert T., *Animals in Migration.* The Macmillan Co., 1970.

Peattie, Donald Culross, *A Natural History of Trees in Eastern and Central North America.* Houghton Mifflin Company, 1970.

Peterson, Roger Tory, *A Field Guide to the Birds: Eastern Land and Water Birds.* Houghton Mifflin Company, 1968.

Peterson, Roger Tory and Margaret McKenny, *A Field Guide to Wildflowers of Northeastern and North-Central North America.* Houghton Mifflin Company, 1968.

Prichard, H. Hesketh, *Through Trackless Labrador.* William Heinemann, 1911.

Rowe, J. S., *Forest Regions of Canada.* Information Canada, 1972.

Russell, Franklin, *The Atlantic Coast.* N.S.L. Natural Sciences of Canada Ltd., 1970.

Saunders, Doris, *Ed.,* "Them Days—Stories of Early Labrador". Vols. I-IV, Labrador Heritage Society and The Old Timers League, 1975-76.

Scott, J. M., *The Land That God Gave Cain.* Chatto and Windus, 1933.

Seton, Ernest Thompson, *Life Histories of Northern Animals.* Vols. I, II, Charles Scribner's Sons, 1909.

Stanwell-Fletcher, Theodora C., *The Tundra World.* Little Brown & Co., 1970.

Tanner, V., *A Bibliography of Labrador.* Helsingfors, 1942.

Townsend, Charles W., *A Labrador Spring.* Dana Estes and Co., 1910.

Wallace, Dillon, *The Lure of the Labrador Wild.* Fleming H. Revell, 1905.

Wild Flowers of Canada. The Montreal Star, 1954.

Yocum, L. E., *Plant Growth.* Jaques Catell Press, 1945.

Acknowledgements

The author and editors of this book wish to thank the following: John Blashill, New York City; Susan Costello, New York City; Roger Craig, Canadian National Railways, Montreal, Canada; C. G. Davis, N.V. "Bonavista", St. John's Newfoundland; Robert Dennis, Department of Energy, Mines and Resources, Ottawa, Canada; Charles Dettmer, Thames Ditton, Surrey; Sidney Dicker, Nain, Labrador; Ken Eaton, Churchill Falls–Labrador Corporation, Churchill Falls, Labrador; William Fitzhugh and Stephen Loring, Department of Anthropology, National Museum of Natural History, Smithsonian Institution, Washington D.C.; Charles Friend, Fisheries and Marine Service, Environment Canada, Ottawa, Canada; Henry Gear, Goose Bay, Labrador; Mr. and Mrs. Horace Goudie, Happy Valley, Labrador; Joseph Kastner, Grandview, New York; David Kennedy, Canadian Broadcasting Corporation, Goose Bay, Labrador; Gerry Lafontaine, Churchill Falls-Labrador Corporation, Montreal, Canada; Ben Ludlow, Northern Labrador Services Division, Government of Newfoundland and Labrador, North West River, Labrador; Dr. James L. Luteyn, Dr. Noel Holmgren, Dr. Richard Prince, Dr. Clark Rogerson, Dr. William C. Steere, Dr. Gary Smith, The New York Botanical Garden, Bronx, New York; Stuart Luttisch, Wildlife Division, Government of Newfoundland and Labrador, Goose Bay, Labrador; Harold Marshall, Gull Island Power Company, Goose Bay, Labrador; Agnes McFarlane, *The Gazette*, Montreal, Canada; John Ski, Colchester, Connecticut; Mr. and Mrs. Ian Strachan, Nain, Labrador; Dr. F. Christian Thompson, Systematic Entomology Laboratory, U.S.D.A., Washington, D.C.; Robert D. Vocke, Jr., Department of Earth and Space Sciences, State University of New York, Stony Brook, New York; Dr. Ronald A. Ward, Walter Reed Army Institute of Research and Medical Entomology Project, Smithsonian Institution, Washington, D.C.; Mr. and Mrs. Chesley Webb, Webb's Bay, Labrador; Henry, Bernard, Bill and Sarah Webb, Nain, Labrador; Isaac Winters, Hopedale, Labrador.

Picture Credits

Sources for pictures in this book are shown below. Credits for the pictures from left to right are separated by commas: from top to bottom they are separated by dashes

Cover–Stephen P. Loutrel. Front end papers 1, 2–John de Visser. Front end paper 3, page 1–W. Eugene Mercer. 2, 3– John de Visser. 4 to 7–Robert Walch. 8, 9–T. C. Dauphine Jr. 10, 11–John de Visser. 12, 13–Candace Cochrane. 18, 19–Map by Hunting Surveys Ltd., London. 22, 23–Candace Cochrane. 26, 27 –Fred Bruemmer. 30–Hope Alexander. 31 –Fred Bruemmer. 32, 33–Hope Alexander. 34–John de Visser. 37–Fred Bruemmer. 38, 39–Candace Cochrane. 40, 41–Dr. W. C. Morgan. 42, 43–John de Visser. 44–Candace Cochrane. 45 to 47– Dr. W. C. Morgan. 51–Fred Bruemmer. 52, 53–Marc Lelo from Jacana, New York. 54–P. A. Milwaukee from Jacana. 57– Dr. W. C. Morgan, 58–Fred Bruemmer. 60 –T. Blagden Jr. 65–Fred Bruemmer. 66– John de Visser. 67–Robert Walch–Candace Cochrane–John de Visser, John de Visser–Paul Johnson–Candace Cochrane–John de Visser. 68–John de Visser. 69–John de Visser–Dr. W. C. Morgan. 70–Paul Johnson from Black Star, New York–Fred Bruemmer. 71– Paul Johnson. 72–Fred Bruemmer. 73– Fred Bruemmer except top centre John de Visser and bottom right Paul Johnson. 74 to 76 John de Visser. 77–John de Visser–Paul Johnson. 81 to 95–*The Lure of the Labrador Wild* by Dillon Wallace, 1905. Copied by Frank Lerner, courtesy of Fleming H. Revell Company, except 83– Map by Walter Johnson. 96–*A Woman's Way Through Unknown Labrador* by Mrs. Leonidas A. Hubbard, Jr., 1908. Copied by Frank Lerner, courtesy of Doubleday and Co., Inc. 98 to 107–Robert Walch. 110–Varin Visage from Jacana. 112 to 114–Robert Walch. 115–E. P. Wheeler II. 116–Robert Walch. 120–Courtesy of New York Historical Society. 122–Map by Elaine Zeitsoff. 124, 125–Fred Bruemmer. 126, 127–John de Visser, Fred Bruemmer. 129–Fred Bruemmer–Walter Winans. 132, 133–John de Visser. 137 to 149–Courtesy New York Historical Society. 155–John de Visser. 158–Ziesler from Jacana. 160–Nils Jensen. 161–Fred A. Curylo from C.P.S. Film Productions. 162–J. P. Varin from Jacana. 166, 167– John de Visser. 171 to 173–Skip Rozin. 174, 175–Paul Johnson. 176, 177–Fred Bruemmer. 178, 179–Skip Rozin.

Index

Figures in italics refer to illustrations

A
Alder, mountain (*Alnus crispa*), 101, *139*
Algae, 118, 119
Alpine arnica (*Arnica alpina*), *70*
Arctic char, 106
Arctic cotton grass (*Eriophorum scheuchzeri*), *64*, 68, *69*
Arctic poppy (*Papaver radicatum*), *73*
Arctic tern, *58*, 124, 130
Ash, black, 153
Aspen, 152
Audubon, John, 120, 124, 130, 136
Audubon, John James, 120, 121, 122, 124, 127, 129, 133, 136, 138, 139, 140, 142-43, 144, 146, 147, 148-49; bird portraits of, 137-49; extracts from Labrador journal of, 120-35
Audubon, Lucy, 136
Auk: great, 136; razor-billed, 122, 123

B
Baffin Bay, 32, 170, *173*
Baffin Island, 31
Bakeapple-berries (*Rubus chamaemorus*), 71, *73*
Bank swallow, 128
Bat, brown, 117
Beach grass, 68
Bear: black, 52, *53*, 54, 59, 159, 163; polar, 48-49, 159, 160, 163
Bear-berries, 100
Beaver River, 87, 90-91, 93
Birch (*Betula*), *74*, *76*; white, 152
Black fly, 85, 110-11, *112*, 117, 119; as specialized feeders, 113-14; bites of, 112; defences against, 111-12; density of swarms, 111; effects on animals, 113; fever caused by, 112; length of active season, 114; life-cycle of, 110-11; limiting effect on human habitation, 111, 112-13; little effect of repellents on, 113
Black-poll warbler, 128
Blake, Donald, 93, *94*
Blake, Gilbert, 93, *94*, 97
Blake, Tom, 90, 92,
"Blow-out", 102, *102*
Blueberries (*Vaccinium uliginosum*), 49, *66*, *70*, 71, 89, 100
Bradore (Bras d'or), *122*, 134

Bunch-berries, 71
Burton, Sir Richard, 80

C
Cabot, William B., 98, 150
Canada jays, 103
Canadian Shield, 22, 35, 111, 114; as world's largest exposed area of Precambrian rock, 35
Canairitock River, *34*
Cape Dyer, 32
Cape Harrison, 25
Cape Makkovik, *133*
Capelin, 28, 62
Caribou, 55, 56, *56*, *88*, 89, 102, 103, 119, 130, 153, 158, 160, 164; adaptation to tundra, 164; migration of, 55, 56, *56*, 102
Caribou moss (*Cladonia alpestris*), 23, 50, *66*, 102, *103*, 105, 152, 153
Cartier, Jacques, 79
Cedar, 153
Chickadees (*Parus hudsonicus*), 100, 110, 132, *139*
Chipmunk, 153
Chokeberry, black (*Aronia melanocarpa*), *139*
Churchill Falls, 108, 118, 156; hydro-electric project, 52, 156
Churchill (formerly Grand) River, 23, 54, 55, 79-80, 152
Cirque, 23, *43*
Cod, 28
Cook, Captain James, 79
Cormorant (*Phalacrocorax carbo*), 128, 130, 131, *144-45*
Cranberry tree (*Viburnum edule*), 71, 89; mountain (*Vaccinium vitis-idaea*), *70*, 100, *100*
Crossbills, 100; white-winged (*Laxia leucoptera*), *139*
Crowberry, black (*Empetrum nigrum*), *73*
Crows, 132
Curlew, 135
Curlew-berries, 71

D
Davis Strait, 31, 63, 170
Deer, 130, 153; *see also* Caribou
Deerfly, 117
Dicker, Gus, 165, 168
Dickie, Eskimo parka, 151
Disappointment Lake, 89, 90

Dog, Eskimo, 165, *166-77*, 168-69; early role played by, 169; fearlessness of, 168; ferocity of, 168; teams of, 165, 168, 169
Dogfish, 62
Dogsled, Arctic, 151, 169
Dolphins, 164
Dragonfly, 118-19
"Drowned shore", 24-25, *26-27*
Ducks: eider, 123, 124, *124*; scoter, 130; velvet, 122

E
Easton, Clifford, 95
Ellesmere Island, 31
Elson, George, 82, 83-97
Erhardt, John Christian, 79
Eric the Red, 25
Erosion, 22-24, 36, *37*, *38-39*, 40, *40-41*, *42-43*, 44-45, 102, 104
"Erratic" rock, 35
Esker, 56
Eskimos, 79, 151, 153, 156-57; settlements in Labrador, 21; government relocation of, 21; *see also* Dog, Eskimo

F
Fernandez, Joao, 79
Fir, balsam, 75, 152
Fireweed (*Epilobium angustifolium*), *73*
Fjord, 23, 31, 35, 40; birth of, *45*
Food chain, 118-19
Foxes, 50, 109, 119; Arctic (white), 152, 159, *160*; red, 152, 159, *161*
Frank's Brook, 98, 103
Frogs, 110

G
Gannet Rock, 120, *148-49*
Gannets (*Marus bassanus*), 120-21, 123-24, *148-49*
Garland Bight, 98
Geese, Canada, 56, 58, 124; migration of, 56, 58
George River, 81, 89
Gillett, Professor J. G., 116
Glaciation, 22-24, 31-32, 35, 36, 40, *40-41*, *42-43*, 44-45
Glaciers, 23, 31-32, 35, 40, *43*; retreat to Arctic, 40; *see also* Glaciation
Goose Bay, 21, 54, 152, 156
Goudie, Allen, 93, *94*
Goudie, Horace, 98-99, 101, 103, 105, 106

Grampus, 98
Grand Banks, 28-29; deposits from
  melted icebergs on, 32
Grand Falls, 80
Grand Lake, 81-82, 84, 91-92, 97
Great tern, 122
Grenfell, Sir Wilfred, 162
Grouse, 110, 131, 156, 160; ruffled
  (partridge), 163, 164; spruce, 50, 154
Gudrid the Fair, 79
Guillemots, 99, 121, 122, 124, 128,
  131
Gulf Stream, 28, 32
Gulf of St. Lawrence, 23, 59, 122
Gulls, 132; Great Black-backed,
  122-24, 131-32
Gyrfalcons (*Falco rusticolus*), 136, *137*

H
Haddock, 28
Halibut, 28
Hamilton Inlet, 83
Happy Valley, 111
Hares, 52; Arctic, 156, 159, 160, 163;
  snowshoe, 49-50, 110, 119, 156, 163
Hebron Eskimo settlement, 21
Hemlock, 153
Heriülf, 25
Heriulfson, Biarni, 25, 78
Herring, 28, 62
Hind, Henry Youle, 79, 94
Horned lark (*Eremophila alpestris*), 135,
  142-43
Horseshoe Rapids, 80
Hubbard, Leonidas, Jnr., 80, *81, 84,*
  91; death of, 94; equipment and
  provisions taken on expedition, 85;
  expedition to Labrador, 80-94;
  privations suffered by, 90-94; routes
  (planned and actual), *82-83*
Hubbard, Mrs. Mina, 96; leads
  Second Hubbard expedition, 95-97
Hudson Strait, 32
Hudson Bay, 21, 22, 24
Hudson's Bay trading post, *81, 82,* 85
Humboldt Glacier, 31

I
Ice Ages, 32, 35, 58, 101; *see also*
  Glaciers
Icebergs, 29, *30, 31,* 32, 170, *171, 172-73,*
  174, 175, 176-77, 178-79; "calving" of,
  32; carried by Labrador Current, 29;
  disintegration of, 29, 32, 170, *176-77;*

height of, 32; movement of, 170;
  origins of, 31; shapes of, 31, 170;
  surface of, 170; wonder of, 29, *30,* 170
Indian House Lake, 114
Irminger Current, 31

J
Jack pine, 153
Jaeger, pomarine (*Stercorarius*
  pomarinus), *147*
James Bay, 97
Juncos, 110

K
Karlsevni, Thorfinn, 79
Kipling, Rudyard, 78, 81, 86
Kittiwakes, *30, 31, 32-33,* 121
Knarr, 25

L
Labrador: as annexe of Newfoundland,
  18, 21; as one of world's last areas to
  be explored in detail, 78; birds of,
  56-58, 120-49; "blow-outs" in, 102;
  climate of, 20, 24, 35, 48-49, 150;
  derivation of name, 79; extent of, 21;
  fauna of, 49-56, 108-10, 157-69; first
  exploration of, 25, 78-97; fish of,
  28, 56-63; flora of, 49, 64-77;
  fogginess of, 28-29; forests in, 23,
  152, 153-54; geological formation of,
  22-24, 36; glaciers in, 40; hazardous
  life in, 156; impression from the air,
  23, 24; insects of, 108, 110-19;
  inhospitable conditions of, 24, 79,
  156-57; lack of amenities and tourist
  attractions in, 25; location of, *18-19,*
  22; "loomy days" of, 20-21; map of,
  18-19; preparations for winter in, 50;
  purity of air in, 24; seasons in, 48-49,
  64; sparse population of, 21;
  topography of, 18, 23; under-snow
  temperatures in, 109; wind chill factor
  in, 151; winter clothing worn in, 150
"Labrador bulldog", *116,* 117
Labrador Current, 25, 28-29, 31, 32,
  48, 100, 170; "cold wall" of, 28;
  extent of, 28; powerful influences of,
  28; rich in mineral salts, 28
Labrador duck, 136
Labrador Peninsula, 18, 21, *26,* 58,
  120, 123
Labrador Plateau, 59, 82
Labrador Sea, 24, 25, 31, 150

Labrador Tea, 49, *103,* 104, 111
Lake Hope, 87
Lake Michikamau, 81, *82,* 87, 89
Lambkill, 104
Larch (*Larix laricina*), 77, 154
Lemmings, 108-09, 110, 119, 159;
  collared, 109, 110; Labrador
  (*Dicrostonyx hudsonius*), 110
Lichens, 66, 67, 156; *Cladonia,* British
  soldier, 67; *Cladonia,* cupped, 67;
  crustose (*Leconora*), 67; Parmelia, 67;
  link (*Xanthoria elegans*), 67, *see also*
  Caribou moss
Lincoln, Tom, 130, 134, 138
"Liveyeres" (*liveheres*), 79
Livingstone, David, 80
Loon, 99, 130, 131; red-throated (*Gavia*
  stellata), *140*
Lost Trail Lake, 87
Low, A. P., *82,* 86; map drawn by, *82*
Lynxes, 50, 114, 119; Canada, 110

M
Mackerel, 28
MacLean, Duncan, 93, *94*
Mallet, Captain Thierry, 48
Maple, 75, 152; red, 75
Martens, 52, 109, 119
Mecatina Harbor, 132
Minks, 50, 109
Moisie River, 58
Montagnais Indians, 79, 82, 86
Moose, 52, *54,* 55; location of, 55
"Moose yard", 54
Moraine, 101
Mosquitoes, 106, 108, 114, *114,* 115, 132;
  capable of killing animals, 116-17;
  egg-hatching by, 117
Mossberries, 89
Mosses, 66; caribou (*Cladonia*
  alpestris), 23, 50, *66,* 102, *103,* 105,
  152, 153; club (*Lycopodium*
  annotinum), 68, 102, *103;*
  Drepanocladus uncinatus, 67; hairy-
  cap (*Polytrichum juniperinum*), 67
Mountain ash, 152
Mountain heath, 104, *105*
Mushroom, brick-topped (*Hypholoma*),
  67

N
Nain, 18, 21, *22,* 24, 55, 98, 114, 156,
  168; population of, 21, 22
Naskaupi Indians, 79, 81, 94, *96*

Naskaupi River, 81-82, 84-86, 93
Natashquan River, 124
New York City, 22, 90
Norsemen, 25
North West River, 50, 81-82, 86, 97
North West River Post, 82-83, 90-94
Northern Lights, 108

O
Osmond, Tom, 56
Osprey, 119
Otter, 119, 130
Owls, 109; great-horned, 109-10; grey, 131; snowy, 110, *110*

P
Partridge, 163-64; *see also* Grouse
Partridge berries, 49
Passenger pigeon, 135
Peccaries, 35
Peregrine falcons, 132, 134, 136
Permafrost, 66, 75, 152
Pine, white, 153
Plover, 134
Poe, Edgar Allan, 50
Pollack, 28
Porpoises, 62, 164
Prichard, H. Hesketh, 114, 156
Ptarmigans, 49, *51*, 110, 131, 160, 163-64; willow (*Lagopus lagopus*), 143
Puffins (*Fratercula arctica*), 128, *147*; Atlantic, *129*

Q
Quebec, province of, 18, 21

R
Rabbit, cottontail, 159
Racoons, 153
Ramah, former Eskimo settlement, 21, 55
Raspberries, 49, 71
Rats, 153
Raven, 50, 132
Razorbills (*Alca torda*), 146
Red-necked diver, 130, 131
Redpolls, 100
Redstarts, 110
Red Wine River, 85-86
Reed-grass (*Calamagrostis canadiensis*), *69*
Ring plover, 128
Roosevelt, President Theodore, 80

Roseroot (*Sedum roseum*), *73*

S
Saksagiak, Mark, 165
Salmon, Atlantic (*Salmo salar*), 58-63, *60*; "alevins", 62; "black", 61; migratory habits of, 58-59, 61-62; "parr", 62; "redd", 61; "smolt", 62; spawning, 59-61; uncanny instinct to return to spawning ground, 60, 63
Sand eels, 62
Sandpiper: speckled, *105*; spotted, 122
Sangamonian Interglacial Stage, 35
Saxifrage (*Saxifraga oppositifolia*), *72*
Schreiber, Ontario, 54
Scoter ducks, surf (*Melanitta perspicillata*), *146*
Seabeach sandwort, *100*
Seal Lake, 86
Seals, 28, 48, 62, 124, 164; harp, 126-27, 164
Sept Isles, 58
Sharks, 28; basking, 62; thresher, 62
Shore lark, 134-35
Shrimp, 62
Skunks, 153
Smallwood Reservoir, 18, 81, 89
Smith Isthmus, 31
Snakes, 153
Snow bunting, *129*
Snowmobiles, 154, 157, 169
Sparrow: fox, 110; Lincoln's (*Melospiza lincolnii*), 138; song, 130; white-crowned, *100*, 101
Sprats, 62
Spruces (*Picea*), *76*, 106; black, (*Picea mariana*), 49, 75, *77*, 102, 103, 153, 154, 155; candelabrum, 154; white, 102, 152
Squirrels, 50, 52, 109; flying, 50, 132; red, 50, 52
Stanley, Henry, 80
St. Lawrence River, 21, 82
Strachan, Mrs. Ian, 117
Strait of Belle Isle, *26*
Strawberry: false, *105*; wild, 105
Susan River, 78, 84-86, 90-91, 93
Swamp laurel, 104, *104*
Swordfish, 28

T
Taiga, 153, 154

Tamaracks, 49, 102, *104*, 106, 153, 154
Thrushes, 110
Titmouse: black-headed, 132; Hudson's Bay, 132
Torngat Mountains, 18, 23; fog over, *46-47*
Trout, 48, 52, 87, 105, 110, 118, 119; speckled, *105*, 119
Tundra, 23, 152, 153, 154, 156, 163, 164, 165

U
Ungava Bay, 81, *96*

V
Valley, hanging, *45*
Varying hare, *see* Hare, snowshoe
Voisey Bay, 98, *99*
Voles, 108-10, 119, 159; red-backed, 109

W
Walch, Robert, 98
Wallace, Dillon, 80-81; author of *The Lure of the Labrador Wild*, 95; member of Leonidas Hubbard's expedition to Labrador, 81-97
Walton, Isaak, author of *The Compleat Angler*, 60
Warblers, 58
Water beetles, 118
Weasels, 49-50, 52, 109, 119, 163
Webb Bay, *154*
Webb, Bernard, 151-52, 154, 156-57
Webb, Bill, 157-58
Webb, Chesley, 159, 162
Webb, Mrs. Chesley, 160
Whales, 28, 29, 164; killer, 62
"White-out" hazard, 24
White pine, 153
Windbound Lake, 89
Winters, Isaac, 168-69
Wolverines, 119, 160, *162*, 163; characteristics of, 162
Wolves, 56, 99, *99*, 100, 119, 157, 166; blue-grey Labrador (*Canus labradorius*), *158*, 159
"Wonderstrands", 79
Woodchuck, 52, 109
Woodpecker, 106, 132

Z
Zoar, former Eskimo settlement, 21

Colour reproduction by P.D.I. Ltd., Leeds, England—a Time Inc. subsidiary.
Filmsetting by C. E. Dawkins (Typesetters) Ltd., London, SE1 1UN.
Printed and bound in Belgium by Brepols S.A.—Turnhout. **XX**